Flexible Integration

Which Model for the European Union?

Alex Warleigh

★ UACES ★

SHEFFIELD ACADEMIC PRESS
A Continuum imprint
LONDON • NEW YORK

Copyright © 2002 Sheffield Academic Press
A Continuum imprint

Published by Sheffield Academic Press Ltd
The Tower Building, 11 York Road, London SE1 7NX
370 Lexington Avenue, New York NY 10017-6550

www.SheffieldAcademicPress.com
www.continuumbooks.com

British Library Cataloguing-in-Publication Data

A catalogue record for this book is available from the British Library

Typeset by Sheffield Academic Press
Printed on acid-free paper in Great Britain by MPG Books Ltd, Bodmin, Cornwall

ISBN 0-8264-6093-3 (paperback)
       0-8264-6092-5 (hardback)

Flexible Integration

Contemporary European Studies, 15

Series Editor
Jackie Gower

Editorial Board
*Clive Archer, Judy Batt,
Stephen George, Michael Newman*

For Christopher Lack, who puts up with my lack of flexibility.
This is one PDA that you can't get away from.

And for the very classy Ms Vice,
who missed out most unjustly last time.

Contents

Tables

Series Foreword

The timing of the publication of the latest book in the Contemporary European Studies series is particularly opportune as the Convention on the Future of Europe launches the debate on the reforms needed to make the EU more effective and more legitimate in the eyes of its citizens. Flexibility will undoubtedly be one of the most controversial ideas that will be debated, with its proponents arguing that it is the only way a much larger and more heterogeneous Union can continue to function effectively, and its opponents fearing that it will undermine the achievements of 50 years of integration. One of the problems in the debate is the lack of general understanding about what flexibility really means and how it has already been applied in a number of specific policy areas. It is hoped, therefore, that this book will make an important contribution to a more informed debate about the options that we have in considering the future of Europe.

The Contemporary European Studies series was launched in 1998 by the University Association of Contemporary European Studies (UACES), the foremost British organization bringing together academics and practitioners interested in the study of contemporary Europe, particularly the institutions and policies of the European Union. The objective of the series is to provide authoritative texts dealing with a wide range of important issues of interest to both those studying and teaching about European integration and professionals wishing to keep up with current developments. In September 2001 the series publisher, Sheffield Academic Press, was acquired by Continuum. Future books will be published under a joint Continuum/UACES imprint with both parties working closely together to develop both the reputation and international sales of the series.

Jackie Gower
Series Editor

Author's Note: The Treaty of Nice

At the time of writing (March 2002), the draft Treaty of Nice (agreed in December 2000) is still to be ratified, following its rejection in a referendum by the people of the Republic of Ireland. It is currently expected that there will be a second Irish referendum, and hoped that the Treaty will be accepted on that occasion, subject to certain clarifications, amendments and, possibly, opt-outs. This would be in keeping with the precedent set by Denmark following its rejection of the Treaty on European Union.

As such is the general assumption, I have referred to the draft Nice Treaty throughout this manuscript as if it were on the statute book, in keeping with the many articles and several books published on that Treaty.

Preface

'I have often been struck by the prevailing view in Community circles that the worst that can happen is any movement towards what is called an *Europe à la carte*. This is not only somewhat odd for someone who likes to make his own choices, but also illustrates that strange Puritanism, not to say masochism, which underlies much of Community action: Europe has to hurt in order to be good' (Professor Ralf Dahrendorf, 'A Third Europe?', Third Jean Monnet Lecture, European University Institute, 26 November 1979).

Acknowledgments

I would like to thank Jackie Gower for her comments on a draft of this book, and for agreeing to publish what she considered to be a controversial manuscript. I would also like to thank Ciarán O'Kelly, Gina Inglis and an unknown scion of the Gower family who helped ensure that the book and I both survived the move from Reading to Belfast, and Mac to PC.

Abbreviations

CC	closer cooperation
CEC	Commission of the European Communities
CFSP	Common Foreign and Security Policy
COREPER	Comité des Représentants Permanents (Committee of Permanent Representatives)
EBRD	European Bank for Reconstruction and Development
EC	European Community
ECB	European Central Bank
ECJ	European Court of Justice
ECSC	European Coal and Steel Community
EEC	European Economic Community
EMU	Economic and Monetary Union
EP	European Parliament
EU	European Union
IGC	intergovernmental conference
MEP	Member of the European Parliament
NATO	North Atlantic Treaty Organization
QMV	qualified majority voting
RRF	Rapid Reaction Force
ToA	Treaty of Amsterdam
ToN	Treaty of Nice
WTO	World Trade Organization

1 |

Understanding Flexible Integration in the European Union

Introduction

Flexibility is emerging as the key dynamic of European integration. The Maastricht, Amsterdam and Nice Treaties have begun to elaborate the basis on which this principle should be operationalized. As the slow process of institutional reform continues, it has become clear that while integration may well 'deepen'—that is, the European Union (EU) may be tasked with greater responsibilities—this is unlikely to occur within a framework of uniformity. Indeed, deepening the integration process may demand flexibility, since member states of the EU differ in their views about what the EU should do, and how much of their autonomy ('national sovereignty') they are willing to trade for the benefits of EU membership. For example, the Schengen agreements on freedom of movement—originally made by the member states as an extra-EU regime—are now part of the Treaty, but they do not apply to the UK or Ireland, and Denmark has negotiated a special, half-in, half-out status. At the macro level, member states continue to differ about whether the EU should become a federal state; at the micro level, they differ about whether the EU should be active in certain policy areas, and if so, about what *kind* of policy it should have. Of course, this is not new: the history of European integration since the creation of the European Coal and Steel Community (ECSC) has been littered with such disputes. Moreover, such differences of opinion are entirely reasonable, since the various member states have divergent reasons for taking part in European integration as well as different policy models and problems.

Over the last decade, however, the member states have begun to shape the integration process in a way which implies an acceptance that these differences may persist rather than wither away. As I make clear below, European integration has always been differentiated rather than uniform; for example, derogations from certain policies have always been granted to member states with special difficulties in applying certain directives (technical incapacities, contradictory relations with third countries and so on). Such derogations were always supposed to be temporary, however, even if many of them lasted for several years. A member state with a derogation agreed to comply eventually, when it became capable of so doing. Since the Treaty on European Union was signed at Maastricht in December 1991, the member states have sanctioned the principle of *permanent opt-outs* from even major policies. Moreover, such opt-outs can be secured not just as a result of incapacity, but because of political will—a deliberate choice not to participate —as has to date been the case for Denmark, the UK and Sweden regarding the single currency. The significance of this is hard to underestimate. It means that the EU will have to cope with being a more complex, and probably less transparent, political system. It also poses challenges to orthodox views of European integration in both academic and practitioner circles, since it makes a state-like outcome to the integration process far less likely, at least as regards the participation of every member state.

Nonetheless, flexibility does not have to be read as a brake on integration. Indeed, the argument of this book is precisely the contrary, namely that flexibility offers the most useful means of balancing different (national) interests and thereby allowing progress to be made for (and in) the EU as a whole. This is for two reasons. First, flexibility enables reluctant member states to opt-out of, rather than oppose, new EU action which they would prefer not to accept, thereby removing the need to use the veto power. Second, given the member states' existing commitment to the single market (all fifteen current members participate fully) and the single currency (now embraced by twelve of the member states), it is unlikely that flexibility would cause the unravelling of key successes of the integration process to date. Instead, it would serve to allow the coexistence of different degrees of (national) commitment to the integration process in different policy regimes, allowing the member states to participate where they so choose. In all likelihood, this would increase the general momentum of the integration process, and might in time lead to its overall upscaling as member states decide to maximize the benefits they accrue from participating in one policy regime by participating in more of those with which it is linked. However, making the most of flexibility requires both a recognition of its problems and also the adoption of different ways of thinking about the goals and structures of European integration (see Chapter 5). Flexibility is not a magic solution to the problems of the Union; indeed, as I make clear in Chapter 4, it poses many difficulties of its own, especially in terms of manageability, transparency and accountability. However, as both a mechanism for managing the EU and a normative approach to its governance, it has much to offer in the ongoing attempt to realize the EU's slogan of 'unity in diversity'.

My intention in this book is to propose a way in which this might be done. Flexibility is seen here as a desirable part of the integration process rather than a problem to be avoided or removed. It is also seen as part of the package of institutional reform which is necessary for the future success of European integration.

The structure of this chapter is as follows. In the next section I explain why and how flexibility has become such a significant feature of the EU. Following this, I set out a typology of flexibility in order to explain the various models which have been put forward over time. I then briefly explore the history of flexibility in the EU and finally I set out and explain the structure of the rest of the book.

Flexibility in the European Union: Deliberate Strategy or Unanticipated Outcome?

As Helen Wallace (2000b) shows, the EU is a highly varied political system, involving five modes of policy making which range from the traditional 'Community Method' and its adaptations to empower the European Parliament (EP) to 'intensive transgovernmentalism' such as the common foreign and security policy (CFSP). The fact that the EU is composed of three 'pillars' exemplifies this variation. The first pillar, the European Community (EC), covers the bulk of EU legislation and sees the EU institutions enjoy their full range of powers. The second pillar is reserved for CFSP, and the third for matters relating to Police and Judicial Cooperation in Criminal Matters (formerly known as Justice and Home Affairs). In pillars 2 and 3, it is the Council of Ministers which dominates, with smaller and sometimes non-existent official roles for the other EU institutions.[1] Furthermore, over time, adding

---

1.   For a guide to the various EU institutions and the nature of decision making in the Union, see Warleigh 2001a, 2001c.

to the EU's competences has often required innovation in the style of policy making. For example, the creation of the European Council to set the direction of the integration process meant that this function was exercised intergovernmentally rather than by the Commission, but it also meant that it was capable of being carried out, thereby filling a gap and helping to take the EU out of a period of relative stagnation (Bulmer 1996). Thus, as the course of integration has run on, the EU has become a very complex and differentiated system, in which policy decisions are made according to different rules according to the issue at hand. Moreover, these rules are themselves capable of adaptation. For instance, the codecision process (which gives the EP and Council of Ministers roughly equal powers over legislation) covers an increasing number of proposals in the first pillar and has been extended to new areas of policy with each Treaty revision since its creation in the Maastricht Treaty.

However, flexibility implies something rather different: the ability of member states to choose not to participate in particular policies no matter how they are made. As such it adds a separate and extra complicating factor to the evolution of EU governance. Given the need to increase the transparency of the EU as part of the reform process, which has itself been given fresh momentum by the declaration that there will be a long run-up to the next round of Treaty reform (scheduled for 2004), there is a clear need to establish the benefits that flexibility may bring to the EU system and, subsequently, whether it has anything to offer this process of reform (see Chapter 5).

Perhaps the principal reason for the ascendancy of flexibility (and one which essentially underlies all other explanations) is its ability to act as a tool for diversity management. The utility of this function cannot be underestimated. As argued above, the member states continue to have different views about both the general role of the EU and particular Union policies: flexibility can be seen as an alternative to qualified majority voting (QMV), which was reintroduced in the Single European Act of 1986 in order to remove the ability of a single member state (or a small number of them) to prevent their partners from taking further action (Gillespie 1997). Of course, there is a difference here: QMV in itself obliges all member states to take part in whatever policy is agreed, whether they voted for it or not; flexibility implies that certain member states will simply opt-out. Nonetheless, it is clear that as an alternative to QMV flexibility allows the integration process to move according to the general will of the member states rather than the wishes of the least inclined to participate (Lamers 1997; de la Serre and Wallace 1997). As such, it can be an essential device for removing opposition; it is almost certain, for example, that the single currency would never have been launched had the UK and Denmark not been allowed to opt out of it by the Maastricht Treaty (the Swedish opt-out was decided later, after their entry to the EU in 1995).

On a related point, flexibility has potential as a means to allow the successful management of the enlargement process. Taking in new member states has always created a wider diversity within the EU; with the prospective entry of over a dozen new members, which each have varying degrees of capacity to implement the full *acquis communautaire* (the body of EU legislation), the EU may have to use flexibility in order to conserve some of its successes. For example, environmental legislation may take many years to apply in certain of the applicant states, meaning that long derogations may be required in order to ensure that the relevant legislation is properly implemented after capacity has been built. Moreover, and moving away from the established approach to enlargement, the EU may have to come to terms with new demands and new considerations voiced by those states currently waiting to join: the latter may seek to opt out of future policies not because they cannot implement them, but because they choose not to, even though in the short to medium term all new member states must implement the full *acquis* as a condition of entry to the EU. Should the enlargement process take longer than predicted, flexibility has another use: it allows applicant states to participate in certain EU regimes for which they are ready, even before formally being a member state of the EU. For example, the Czech Republic, Poland and Hungary are members of NATO and are thus involved with the EU's new Rapid Reaction Force; there is no *a priori* reason why this principle could not be extended to other policy areas.

At a more micro level, flexibility has already served as a means of reconciling the different goals and views of member states concerning a given piece of legislation. Bailey (1999) shows how environmental legislation allows member states to use different tools to meet the agreed common goal, and also to allow a single piece of legislation to meet different objectives—in his study of the packaging waste directive, Bailey shows how member states used flexibility to reconcile diverging key goals (namely preserving the single market emphasis on free trade and ensuring environmental protection standards). As such, flexibility can be a means by which member states are able to agree legislation despite significant differences of opinion, serving as 'a way to find compromise and avoid log jam' (Stubb 1997: 47).

A further reason why flexibility has risen up the EU agenda is its ability in principle to delegitimize or remove the need for cooperation by member states outside the EU structures. This allows the improvement of EU efficiency (Dewatripont *et al.* 1995). If member states are allowed to opt out of policies they do not support, and by the same token groups of member states who share common objectives are allowed to pursue them as a matter of EU policy, then there is little justification for pursuing such policies bi- or multi-laterally by other means. The Schengen accords are a key example here. Originally agreed in 1985 as a means of moving the EU towards one of its key objectives—freedom of movement—they were set up outside the Treaty as a result of opposition from certain member states (notably the UK) to allowing this legislation the full force of EC law. The incorporation of the accords into the Treaty as a result of the 1997 Amsterdam Summit has improved the coherence and implementation of policy in that area and enabled the EU to make progress in delivering one of its main provisions on citizenship; the corollary was the opt-outs for the UK, Ireland and Denmark.

Perhaps more controversially, flexibility can be read as part of the solution to the democratic deficit. If the process of democratization in the EU is seen neither as an exercise in state-building (the traditional pro-European view) nor as one of repatriating as many powers as possible to the member states (the Eurosceptic view), but rather as one which accepts the EU's status as an evolving political system with deep roots in its component member states, it is possible to conceive democratization in a way which sees flexibility as a positive advantage (Warleigh 2002). This is because flexibility rests on the principle of managed, but respected, diversity—the maintenance of which is itself a key challenge of the EU.

If these are the reasons usually put forward to set out the benefits of flexibility, it remains to explain in more detail why the member states have agreed to abandon their traditional emphasis on more uniform approaches. The principal issue here is whether flexibility results from a conscious strategy (either to contain or unleash the integration dynamics) or from an accumulation of pressures based on responses to relatively isolated incidents and problems. The more important theoretical aspects of this issue are discussed in Chapter 2.

Several commentators argue that flexibility is a means by which member states have sought to limit further integration. In this view, its appearance as an accepted feature of the Treaty is part of a general strategy evident throughout the 1990s by which the larger member states sought to reduce actual recourse to QMV, challenge the supremacy of EC law, 'repatriate' certain of the powers of the Commission, and shift the focus of EU policy making from binding legislation towards 'soft policy' reliant on voluntary compliance (Devuyst 1999; Moravcsik and Nicolaidis 1999). This view reflects the fears of legal scholars expressed several years earlier that *political* use of flexibility, as opposed to that built into EC legislation (its differentiated application and implementation patterns, its reliance upon directives rather than entirely binding regulations), would be at best superfluous and at worst a means to undermine EC law as a force for integration (Ehlermann 1984). Flexibility can also be seen as a substitute for 'proper' reform of the EU, as it avoids making definitive binding decisions about the end product and structure of integration (Chaltiel 1998).

It is certainly no accident that flexibility has gained greater salience at a stage in the integration process in which Treaty reform is unadventurous compared with the great steps taken in the Single Act and at Maastricht, and in which the supremacy of EC law has been repeatedly questioned by national courts. However, there are other factors which have also been important in causing the shift towards flexibility. After all, certain member states have argued throughout the history of integration—or at least during moments of perceived stagnation—that flexibility is a means of deepening the integration process (Tindemans 1976; Lamers 1997). It cannot thus be taken for granted that all member states seeking, or agreeing to, flexibility do so in order to provide impediments to integration. Moreover, it cannot be assumed that its enshrinement in the Treaty is solely the result of deliberate member state choices, although some scholars argue forcefully that it is necessary to understand how and why powerful member states may support the idea as a means of ensuring their ability to assert leadership of the Union (Pedersen 2000).

Schmitter (1996) argues that the EU is part of the European 'condominio', that is, it is the evolving and internally differentiated core of an overlapping system of organizations set up for the governance of the

whole continent of Europe.[2] This condominio involves many regimes
covering different (sets of) policies—security, human rights, free trade
and so on—with different sets of member states. It evolves over time in
response to both internal and external pressures—particularly the
collapse of communist regimes in Central and Eastern Europe in 1989.
According to Schmitter, while this is clearly a deliberate strategy for
ensuring the governability of the continent, the exact configuration of
the condominio results not from a single clear design but rather from
accumulated pressures and responses to particular crises or opportunities. Thus, it is, in historical institutionalist terms, path dependent, the
'result of a series of strategic compromises and gambits, of policy-
driven sectoral initiatives, and of accommodations of new geopolitical
forces' (Walker 1998: 374). A further argument along similar lines
results from an analysis of the method used to promote further integration by the originators of the process, who hoped that over time the
Union would grow to statehood not by the signing of a federal treaty at
the outset but organically by the process of 'spillover'—the perceived
need to protect and maximize the benefits of integration in one policy
area by integrating those to which it was linked (Haas 1964; 1968). In
fact, integration has been a fundamentally contested process in which
the potential for spillover has been somewhat truncated by member
states' 'defence' of their autonomy. Thus, although integration has
unquestionably deepened, it has done so elliptically and as a result of
entrepreneurship (the creation and exploitation of opportunities by
actors seeking influence, often but not exclusively from the EU institutions) and coalition building, particularly in the European Council and
Council of Ministers. Flexibility reflects this fundamentally contested
nature of the integration process, whose dynamics are extremely
unlikely to produce a uniform outcome.

Thus, flexibility's advent can be explained *both* as a result of member
states' determination to deepen integration in their own interests *and* as
a product of the contested evolution of the EU (i.e. its ongoing but
idiosyncratic development). This dual explanation also helps explain
why the translation of flexibility into the Treaty has so far been both
ambiguous and cautious (see Chapter 3).

   2.   See also the similar concept of 'network governance' (Kohler-Koch and
Eising 1999).

A Typology of Flexibility

One of the difficulties of seeking to understand flexibility is the diversity of models and concepts which it covers as an umbrella term.[3] So different are these models that in fact it is increasingly common for one of them—multi-speed integration—to be accepted as an inevitability, while another—the à la carte model—is almost universally derided.[4] Moreover, the principal method by which flexibility has been incorporated into the Treaty—the provisions of the Amsterdam and Nice Treaties on 'closer cooperation'[5]—simultaneously evinces aspects of all three of the main models. Thus, while it is important to understand what the Treaty actually says (and why), it is also vital to have an understanding of the models on which it draws. In addition, it must be remembered that, just like the EU, flexibility—or at least closer cooperation—is subject to evolution, and that consequently its present hybridity may be re-examined.[6]

A further complication is that flexibility works differently in each pillar of the EU. In the first pillar, the Commission has a *de facto* veto right in that it must approve all proposed closer cooperation measures. If co-decision applies to legislation produced through closer cooperation, the EP has a similar power, as it must approve such proposals by the assent procedure (i.e. it can approve or disapprove, but not amend, the proposal). The scope for flexibility is narrow in pillar 2, and all power is with the Council of Ministers (using QMV). In pillar 3 the procedure is similar, but the scope is somewhat wider.

Table 1.1 is a typology of the three main models of flexibility. There are two main distinctions between these models: the degree of differentiation they envisage, and the period of time for which this differentiation is considered acceptable.

3. See Stubb 1996 for a thorough exploration of the different terms and models related to flexibility.

4. As is made clear in Chapter 2, the present book is an exception in this regard.

5. Like Eric Philippart (2001), I use the initial translation of 'co-opération renforcée' rather than the currently in vogue 'enhanced cooperation', in order to avoid confusion when using abbreviations—hence, 'CC' rather than the otherwise necessary 'EC'.

6. For a detailed examination of the evolution of closer cooperation, see Chapter 3.

Table 1.1: Models of Flexibility

Model	Main cause of differentiation	Vision of integration
Multi-speed	Inability to implement policy (short term)	Policy regimes with different members; laggards commit to catch up over time
Concentric circles	Inability to implement policy (long term)	Various tiers of member states around a hard core
À la carte	Choice not to participate in certain policies	Policy regimes with different memberships over the long term

Multi-speed integration is essentially a means to conceptualize what is in any case standard practice in European integration, namely the implementation of policies initially only by those member states immediately capable of so doing, and the subsequent implementation of the relevant policies by member states without the initial capacity as soon as they have it. In this model, the main variable is thus capacity, not will; all member states agree that they will eventually adopt the same policies. In certain variants of this model (Tindemans 1976), those member states which launch the policy have a duty to help their colleagues catch up. Thus, multi-speed models are, at heart, solidaristic, and differentiation between the member states is considered a temporary and unfortunate necessity. An example is the numerous derogations from EU policy granted to many member states throughout EU history.

The concentric circles model, however, is predicated on the assumption that certain member states are likely to be effectively incapable of adopting certain policies for long periods of time, perhaps for ever.[7] It advocates that integration should thus be reorganized into divisions rather like a football league: the EU's policies should be divided into discrete sections, and each member state should then join the division which corresponds to the degree of EU legislation with which it is able (or perhaps willing, although the main criterion is capacity rather than

7.   I do not use the term 'variable geometry' in this book because it has been subject to many different interpretations. It is often a synonym for flexibility itself, as pointed out by Junge (1999: 38-40), but is also used by many scholars to denote what I here call the 'concentric circles' model (Stubb 1996; Dewatripont *et al.* 1995). To avoid confusion, I avoid the term altogether.

will) to comply. An example is the plan for a 'hard core' of member states composed of France, Germany and Benelux (Lamers 1997). It would be possible for a member state to gain promotion into a higher 'division' if it makes the necessary improvements in capacity. Nonetheless, this model differs from the multi-speed approach in that it both expects and advocates more or less permanent differentiation between the member states. Moreover, it does so over a range of policy areas, whereas in the multi-speed model differentiation between member states is likely to be related to individual policies rather than entire sections of the *acquis*. To date, the concentric circles model has been applied to the EU more often in theory than in practice, since although both the UK and Denmark are outside both the Schengen legislation and the single currency, they are joined by Ireland in the first case, and Sweden in the second. Further, their non-participation in both policies is through choice, not incapacity.

À la carte versions of flexibility are in some ways a mixture of the first two, although they have a very important key difference. Both multi-speed and concentric circle models take capacity to implement EU policy as the basis for differentiation between member states; à la carte models are predicated on *political will*, that is, express choices not to participate. As in multi-speed models, à la carte approaches advocate a pattern of core-periphery relations which differs according to the policy issue, and not a formal separation of the EU into different and essentially permanent tiers of membership. However, like concentric circles models, à la carte approaches are prepared to accept such patterns of differentiation as permanent, although at any time a non-participant member state could change its mind and accept further parts of the *acquis*. While it would be inaccurate to claim that the EU already fits this model, it has certainly adopted it on occasion, as indicated by the UK opt-out from much social policy (subsequently abandoned by London on the election of the Labour government of 1997).

It is clear that the EU has not yet adopted any model of flexibility as a sole reference point. As stated above, and demonstrated in Table 1.2, simultaneous recourse to all models is apparent in the arrangements made for 'closer cooperation'.

The triggering mechanism for closer cooperation varies according to the pillar structure, meaning that right at the outset the situation is confused. Because the Commission and EP have significant powers over the launch of flexibility in pillar 1, this implies a multi-speed model on the assumption that both these institutions will seek to 'protect' both small states and the general 'European' interest, thereby insisting that no hard core of member states will emerge. In pillars 2 and 3, the preponderance of the Council, voting by QMV, implies that different clusters of member states will cooperate according to policy issue. This is because QMV requires a more widely spread agreement than a simple majority, and thus is likely to prevent the emergence of a single, tightly bound set of leading member states. However, the fact remains that the quorum for all closer cooperation measures—eight member states—is far less than a qualified majority and only temporarily constitutes a simple majority: indeed, after the next round of enlargement, the quorum may require less than a third of the member states.

Table 1.2: Closer Co-operation and Models of Flexibility

Variable	What the treaty says[a]	Corresponding model
Triggering mechanism	Varies according to pillar	Multi-speed (pillar 1); à la carte (pillars 2 and 3)
Quorum	Eight member states (not a majority)	Concentric circles
National veto over launch?	No (except in pillar 2)	À la carte
Present in all pillars?	Yes (but limited in pillar 2)	Concentric circles
Uniform across all pillars?	No	À la carte
A means to add new competences to the EU?	No	Multi-speed
Can laggards join the vanguard?	Yes	Multi-speed

a. In this table I refer to the *acquis* as it would stand after ratification of the Nice Treaty (still pending ratification at time of writing).

In direct contradiction of the previous point, this implies that a 'concentric circles' future for the EU cannot yet be ruled out: given that by meeting the criteria for the single currency the economic compatibility of those in the Euro-zone has been officially sanctioned, a core group of generally pro-integration member states could feasibly coalesce around the Franco-German axis.[8] However, a potential barrier to the emergence of such a core group is raised by the fact that closer co-operation cannot be used to add new competences to the Union preserve. Indeed, the Treaty insists that flexibility must be an approach used as a 'last resort', must be accessible to non-participants if they change their minds, and must respect the existing *acquis* in terms of both economic and social cohesion and competition policy. This implies limited recourse to closer cooperation, and the use of a multi-speed model.

Nonetheless, the fact that apart from in pillar 2 there is no unanimity requirement for the launch of closer cooperation implies that the à la carte approach cannot be ruled out either. This is partly because no member state can use its veto unilaterally to prevent either multi-speed integration or even consignment to a lower 'division' of membership. It is also because if no hard core does emerge, the low quorum require-ment means that overlapping core groups are likely, with membership varying according to policy area. This possibility is brought closer by the differentiation in flexibility across the pillars; not only do the deci-sion rules vary, but so does the likely membership of the respective 'cores' in each pillar—for instance, the UK will probably be at the heart of the increasing cooperation in pillar 2 but may well remain outside the single currency for a considerable time. As a result, it is not yet possible to assess which variant of flexibility the EU will eventually adopt; current evidence based on reading the Treaty provisions indi-cates a multi-speed model, but does not preclude either of its rivals. This view also emerges from an understanding of how flexibility has been enacted to date in the integration process.

A Brief History of Flexibility: Practice and Principle[9]

Although official acceptance and recognition of flexibility as a *prin-ciple of EU governance* has only recently been forthcoming, differ-entiated integration has long been the distinguishing mark of *practice*

---

8.   Such a group would probably also include a selection of the other founding states (Benelux, Italy) and, if neutrality is not seen to pose a problem, Ireland, Austria and Finland. Spain and Portugal might also feature in such a core if problems with regional policy are resolved.

9.   A detailed examination of the evolution of flexibility between the Treaties of Amsterdam and Nice is provided in Chapter 3.

in what is now the EU. William Wallace (1990) points out that different kinds of policy area have followed highly divergent integrative paths, and indeed some of them have yet to fall into EU hands at all. In general, economic integration has been more advanced than the political and social variants, although since Maastricht this gap has closed noticeably. Furthermore, flexibility has long been a response to the problem of enlargement, going back to its first instance in 1973 (accession of Denmark, Ireland and the UK) (Junge 1999). The *Cassis-de-Dijon* ruling by the European Court of Justice (ECJ) meant that harmonization of legislation was not necessary to construct the single market; instead, the latter could be based on sets of common minimum standards, thereby legitimating the persistence of what continue to be often highly diverse national practices around a common policy core. Moreover, the fact that most EU legislation is in the form of directives enhances this variation, since member states are free to implement the agreed framework in their own ways rather than according to a single pattern. As stated above, the persistence of multiple derogations from pieces of legislation for many member states has meant that in reality the EU has never been a uniform system or a 'level playing-field'.

In the 1970s, calls for a turn towards the principle of à la carte integration were made, although they were not common (Armand and Drancourt 1970; Dahrendorf 1979). This was a response to the perceived stagnation of the EU at the time, itself largely a result of de Gaulle's robust defence of French sovereignty in the 'empty chair' crisis of 1965, when the French Head of State prevented a shift to QMV and the partial empowerment of the EP. This model of flexibility was seen to marry national sovereignty and deeper integration successfully by allowing variable degrees of participation in the collective EU enterprise, and thereby enabling integration to proceed where a majority of member states so chose. The failure to adopt such an approach was subsequently diagnosed as the main cause of the (then) EEC's continuing failure to develop (Taylor 1983). However, although the orthodox line on flexibility was that it equated to a failure of the integration process, and should thus be avoided (Monnet 1978), several attempts to shift the EU towards a multi-speed model were made— again as a response to perceived stagnation resulting from both the inability of the member states to agree on policy goals and the pressures of enlargement (Tindemans 1976). Given that multi-speed models of integration are designed to be temporary and to encourage solidarity between non-participants and those 'in the loop', it was considered by many EU actors and scholars to be a useful tactic, since it would allow the more developed states to exert a positive influence on the others both by example and by explicit aid. This would build overall capacity and encourage solidarity. Thus, certain 'good Europeans' argued that the ends could justify what they perceived to be rather unpleasant means (Ehlermann 1995; Maillet and Vélo 1994).

As a principle of governance, however, flexibility was destined to remain under-used and under-determined. This was because 'awkward' Europeans held a far more cautious view. The UK government, for instance, was deeply opposed to any kind of flexibility throughout the 1980s, considering that it would lose influence were flexibility to become a principle of EU governance. Preserving official uniformity meant that the UK could determine the speed of the entire integration process at the macro level, and thereby ensure that it did not 'spill-over' into unwanted policy areas (Taylor 1996). Although the UK subsequently shifted strategically towards an à la carte view at the time of the Maastricht Treaty, this reflected not so much a wish for deeper integration, but rather a rearguard attempt to counter German support for a multi-speed approach and French support for a concentric circles model, themselves borne of frustration with the speed of integration in what may historically appear the halcyon period of Euro-enthusiasm (Taylor 1996). The Maastricht Treaty was supposed to elaborate plans for both economic and political union as a response to the collapse of communism in Central and Eastern Europe and the resultant end of the Cold War. Germany and France, together with certain other member states, were prepared to unleash flexibility, if need be, to achieve economic and political union, at least for a vanguard group (in the French model). The UK was not, both because it did not want integration to extend that far, and because it feared loss of influence if it fell outside the leading group. Hence the Maastricht Treaty produced the pillar structure, selected opt-outs and limited progress towards political union, while including a detailed timetable and set of criteria for monetary union. Flexibility was not elaborated as a principle, but was significantly altered as a practice by the innovation of the opt-out (the deliberate choice not to participate) (Laursen 1997).

As a principle, then, it was only with the Amsterdam Treaty that flexibility was in any way clearly articulated. However, even with the Nice Treaty it remains confused and ambiguous. The Amsterdam variant of closer cooperation was widely considered to be too clumsy to operationalize, thanks to the existence of multiple vetoes on the triggering mechanism, comprising a cautious quasi-constitutionaliz-ation of the principle of flexibility rather than a serious attempt to make its potential clear either normatively or managerially (Shaw 1998; Warleigh 2002). With the Nice Treaty, closer cooperation was made slightly less ambiguous, although it remains confused (see the section above): member states appear to have considered this partial, cautious change necessary in the face of further enlargement, which prospect also made them less wary about being consigned to the second or third 'division' of the Union given the anticipated long-term relative incapacity to implement the full *acquis* of the likely entrants (Philippart 2001). In addition, the last round of treaty reform abolished the national veto over the triggering of closer cooperation. Flexibility has thus been confirmed and partially clarified as a principle of EU governance; moreover, it has been both facilitated and transformed as a practice.

Structure of this Book

This introductory chapter is designed to clarify why flexibility has become so central to European integration. It explains the advent of 'closer cooperation' as well as the persistence and transformation of other practices of flexibility, providing both a typology of the main models of flexibility and a brief history of its role in EU governance. Chapter 2 takes a different trajectory while continuing to set flexibility in context by locating it in the rich body of literature dedicated to integration theory. Chapter 3 analyses the first elaboration of flexibility as a principle of EU governance, namely 'closer cooperation'. It traces the latter's development from Amsterdam to Nice, providing a detailed analysis and explanation of its emergence in the first of these treaties and revision in the second. Chapter 4 examines the problems of flexibility, focusing on issues such as legitimacy, manageability and transparency. Finally, Chapter 5 sets out the means to solve at least some of these problems and ensure that flexibility can contribute positively to the process of European integration.

2 |

Theorizing Flexibility: The Return of Functionalism?

Introduction: Flexibility, Integration Theory and the Normative Gap in EU Study

Integration theory has been in a period of difficult revision for over a decade. As a result of their inadequacies, orthodox approaches such as neofunctionalism and intergovernmentalism have been increasingly questioned; new approaches drawing on comparative politics rather than international relations have been articulated; and the tasks integration theorists set themselves have fundamentally altered as a result. The ambitious goals of the early 'grand theories' are, for the most part, no longer fashionable; instead, scholars tend to attempt to understand particular aspects of the EU system, and in some cases, following the lead of Peterson (1995), to link various theories together in an attempt to generate a more holistic understanding (Warleigh 2000a). Against this backdrop, normative issues are also increasingly foregrounded in contemporary academic study of the EU. The middle-range empirically driven theories of the 1990s are now often complemented by explicitly normative enquiries, such as what the EU should do and what kind of structures it should have. Much of this work is being done by political theorists and legal scientists, searching for a new European constitutional order (see, e.g., Weiler 1995; Bellamy and Castiglione 1997; Curtin 1997; Weale and Nentwich 1998; Shaw 1999). Others urge a return to meta-theory, asking that scholars emphasize issues of democracy and legitimacy in order to generate operationalizable models of EU reform (Chryssochoou 2000). Relatedly, others deploy a thorough sociology of knowledge approach in order to contextualize and refine our understandings of the major schools of thought in integration theory (Rosamond 2000a; 2000b).

In this chapter I add to this 'normative turn' by suggesting that it offers the opportunity to remove functionalism from the periphery of EU study. Flexibility, after all, is not just managerial, but normative: it implies that different policy régimes *should* function in different ways. In the search for a means of democratizing the EU, it is likely that new or at least different models of democracy will be needed (Schmitter 2000); indeed, it is in many ways the refusal (or at least the inability) to look beyond conventional 'frames' of democracy which has both contributed to the diagnosis of the 'democratic deficit' and hindered its resolution (Kohler-Koch 2000; Warleigh 2002). Functionalism offers just such a different 'frame', arguing that integration must be seen not as a power struggle between national and supranational actors over the formation of a new transnational state, but rather as a set of 'instances where like interests meet and combine into functionally and territorially diversified "clusters of co-operation"' (Tuytschaever 1999: 252). It thus points towards a non-hierarchical European political system based on overlapping sub-systems, with judicial (or political) authorities in place to solve any 'boundary disputes' and ensure administrative coordination (Tuytschaever 1999).[1]

Functionalism also stresses the gradual process of mass attitudinal change through rational debate based on action taken to secure, and respond to, peaceful economic development (Taylor 1978a; 1975). This is extremely pertinent to a Union mired in the democratic deficit. Moreover, it suggests a way out of the latter impasse, arguing that integration must be about 'encouraging participation in the tackling of specific tasks and service industries' (Taylor 1978b: 240) rather than encouraging sporadic mass voting in elections as a tool of state- or federation-building.[2] Functionalism thus provides a solid ethical and normative basis for flexible integration, a phenomenon that is often treated by integrationists as shameful foot-stamping by national governments, and by intergovernmentalists as proof of the continued defence of national sovereignty.[3] I maintain that despite the continuing

---

1.   The issue of how far functionalism can be 'political' is discussed in the final section of this chapter.

2.   For an intriguing parallel, see Wiener's (1998) advocacy of 'citizenship practice'.

3.   This is a key difference from the traditional Community Method, which espoused an elitist and non-participatory albeit welfare-driven 'ethics of integration' (Bellamy and Warleigh 1998).

limits of the 'closer cooperation' provisions even after Nice, flexibility can best be read as an exercise in functionalist organization: functionalism advocates a polycentric, variegated, non-hierarchical method of transnational governance much like the emerging flexible Union. Consequently, functionalism also has a degree of explanatory capacity to buttress its normative power. Moreover, its stress on the need for evolutive governance (Mitrany 1933; 1944; 1971; Pentland 1975) is germane to the developing Europolity.

The structure of the chapter is as follows. In the next section, I rehearse the main arguments of functionalism, and show how it links with the 'normative turn' in EU scholarship. Following this, I develop further the case for the rehabilitation of functionalism and set out a manner in which this might be done more successfully than by the neofunctionalist scholars of the 1950s–1970s. The fourth section focuses on the issue of flexibility, discussing intergovernmentalist readings of closer cooperation;[4] in the final section I conclude by presenting a functionalist account of flexibility and argue that it is the most satisfactory from both normative and explanatory perspectives.

What Does Functionalism Entail? A Brief Guide to the Principal Tenets

The Problem of Modernity and the International Arena
Functionalists locate their theory in an analysis of two major issues: the nature of domestic politics and the condition of the international arena. They have two primary objectives: the maximization of public welfare, and the securing of international peace. For functionalists, the two goals are inextricably linked.

Mitrany (1975: 245-46) argued prophetically that modern governance is slipping beyond the liberal democratic blueprint thanks to three related phenomena. First, the rise of executive power, which makes parliaments less salient in practice than in theory. Second, the reshaping of citizen involvement in public policy: instead of direct individual action, citizens increasingly rely on shaping policy indirectly, that is through the efforts of government actors seeking re-election to produce outcomes in keeping with, or at least not too far away from, perceived public preferences. Third, the growth of the (welfare) state, which has

---

4.   For excellent general guides to integration theory, see Rosamond 2000b and O'Neill 1996.

provided social protection at the cost of far-ranging interference in the erstwhile private sphere. As a result, domestic governance is both 'post-parliamentary' (Andersen and Burns 1996) and subject to an increased level of state control. In addition, what we would now call globalization has undermined the ability of states to erect barriers between their peoples; social, as well as economic, life has become part of an 'intricate network of cross-national services and exchanges' (Mitrany 1975: 260). The state is thus problematized as caught in a dilemma: internally increasing its power, while suffering external pressures which undermine it. For functionalists, this creates the primary problem in need of solution: modern life is so complicated that it must be organized, but such organization cannot come from the state, given its tendency to develop undemocratically at the national level and its inability to protect the citizen externally (Mitrany 1933).

Matters are complicated by the nature of the international arena. Functionalists consider the default nature of international relations to be dangerously anarchic, the result of too great an emphasis on national sovereignty and too little concentration on international collective action. Put simply, functionalists consider that the existence of national states automatically creates divisions in international society, separating 'us' from 'them' (Mitrany 1933). War is not inevitable; but the traditional primary means of seeking to prevent it, the principle of the rule of law, is inherently flawed since it rests on a fiction: the supposed equality and sovereignty of all states. For functionalists, this supposition is erroneous on three counts. First, there are obvious demonstrable differences in resources, wealth and power between states, themselves subject to change over time. Second, state sovereignty is limited, since economic interdependence and international treaties limit it factually while the multiple loyalties and identities of the citizen circumscribe it normatively. Third, by focusing on 'sovereignty', we legitimize states' insistence on their rights instead of focusing on their responsibilities—to deliver, or at least allow, good governance to their citizens (Mitrany 1933). As a result, the discourse of the rule of law, as traditionally configured, risks reifying an international order which fails to promote the welfare of the citizen. Moreover, it also legitimizes attempts by national governments to control 'their' economies, increasing the likelihood of inter-state conflict given the context of economic interdependence.

The Functionalist Model of International Organization
Consequently functionalists urged the development of a very different
international order. They argued that two factors are necessary for
successful international governance: economic cooperation (Mitrany
1933) and an agreement to submit to common structures of government, each devoted to a particular (set of) functional task(s) rather than
a specific territorial area. Instead of replicating the nation state by
attempting to form a monolithic world government, functionalists
sought to erect a network of overlapping agencies, in which nation
states became effectively obsolete (Hancock 1941–44;[5] Mitrany 1944).
Ultimate political authority would reside with the citizens of the globe
in terms of decisions of a 'constitutional' nature; otherwise, law would
be made by the various functional agencies with coordination ensured
by the existence of an international judiciary and a special body elected
by a world congress. Accountability of each agency would be ensured
through the election of sector-specific assemblies (Hancock 1941–44;
Mitrany 1971). The precise constitution of each functional agency
would alter over time, and there would be no need to ensure that all
agencies had the same structures. Relations between states would be
regulated by functional need rather than their relative strength; functionalists placed great emphasis on devolution and what we would now
call subsidiarity (Mitrany 1933). Within each agency, states would not
insist on equal representation and input but would rather allow those
with specific expertise/capacity to take the lead in the name of the
international community on a quid pro quo basis and in the context of
the international assemblies and judiciary (Mitrany 1975). Thus, there
would be a reduced temptation to indulge in log-rolling (as opposed to
consensus-formation), since states with no real stake in an issue would
not take part in its regulation.[6]
   In terms of mechanisms for the operation of this global network,
functionalists stress negotiation as a means of conflict resolution, with

---

   5.   The precise date of publication is the subject of debate. Hancock claimed to
predate Mitrany, but this has not, to my knowledge, been proved.
   6.   It must be acknowledged that in this respect functionalism is vulnerable to
criticism on environmental grounds. For example, while Switzerland may have no
direct stake in the protection of the rainforests, it does have an interest in preventing
the ozone depletion facilitated by their destruction. While it is helpful to treat issues
separately, certain policy imperatives may well require mainstreaming.

minimal use of imposed settlements in order to avoid mass resentment. Given the ongoing process of social change, conflicts would need to be addressed in an ongoing and evolutionary manner. As a result, functionalists place great trust in the use of common institutions which provide the arenas for such deliberation, but lay no real emphasis on a prior sense of socio-political community since it is deliberation which will eventually produce such common bonds (Mitrany 1975). Functionalists do not advocate a detailed blueprint of international organization beyond the above description, since the pressures which lead to joint action are seen as neither inherently likely to produce a given *finalité politique* nor able to mould cooperation to a pre-selected model once the new functional agency is up and running, given the open-ended nature of the deliberative process (Pentland 1975). However, they do stress the deliberative and evolutionary method. Attempts to build a new federal state are misguided and retrograde since they seek to replicate the structures of the state in the absence of a supporting popular will[7] (Taylor 1978b); instead, those seeking to strengthen international cooperation must simply be tortoises rather than hares.

Nonetheless, functionalists do have a solid idea of the mechanism of progress in international cooperation. In functionalist thought, there is no separation between 'high' and 'low' politics in the Realist sense. Instead, international cooperation in individual issue areas is either controversial or not according to a more nebulous criterion: public opinion.[8] The latter can be expected to change over time, gradually 'eroding the vestiges of particularism' (Pentland 1975: 21). Clearly, functionalists as well as neofunctionalists have a certain concept of spillover. However, as Taylor (1978b) points out, the two versions are very different. Functionalists see the crucial catalyst as changes in public opinion, driven by perceived failures of national governments to provide welfare; neofunctionalists stress deliberate engineering by (supranational) élites and interest groups. Moreover, unlike their revisers, functionalists do not assume that governments always need to

7.   See the final section of this chapter for a discussion of the implications of this point for the application of functionalism to the study of the EU.

8.   It is worth noting here that public opinion appears to diverge significantly from that of both most politicians and most academics by resisting European integration in some matters of 'low' politics, such as health and safety at work, and actively desiring it in at least some issues of 'high' politics, such as defence and foreign policy (Blondel, Sinnott and Svensson 1998).

be lured into cooperation with each other. Instead, they consider that, once started, a process of integration causes a certain degree of ideational change in governments. What actors perceive to be important simply changes as welfare becomes prioritized and instances of successful cooperation provide a model for future collaboration. Importantly, governments remain powerful and may choose either not to take part in the new cooperation measure or to contest the policy of the relevant international agency. However, this is considered to become less likely over time, as 'the issue of sovereignty becomes irrelevant to the important issues in the emerging world society' (Taylor 1978b: 245). Consequently, functionalism can explain both the increasing scope of cooperation in Europe as well as its continuing contested nature, although functionalism would expect such contestation to decline over time as the Union matures.

The Role of the State, and Constitutional Issues
Functionalists have no love for the nation state. While accepting its obstinacy, they consider it normatively inferior to global functional governance, and thus support international law and economic interdependence as evidence of the state's weakening (Mitrany 1975: 94-95). Moreover, as stated above, functionalists consider that pluralism—both internally and outside the structure of the state—defeats the value and indeed the feasibility of national sovereignty. States are seen as artificial constructs subject to change and flux in terms of their geographical extent, powers and standing in the international pecking order (Mitrany 1933). Who would classify Egypt, Persia, Greece or Britain as superpowers now despite their pre-eminence at various stages of history? Is the regulatory state the same kind of entity as the totalitarian model? And so on. For functionalists, states are a distraction from the real issue: the maximization of welfare for all citizens.

As a result, functionalists place politics into a different context. They do not ignore or downplay the importance of politics in the international arena. Instead, they seek to detach it from the idea of the state, as is illustrated by the functionalist approach to the issue of the constitution. Functionalists consider *fixed* constitutions to be a device for the creation and preservation of a state structure (Mitrany 1965); like all else in politics, constitutional arrangements should, in the functionalist view, *evolve*. However, this does not mean that functionalists consider that a European/world constitution will emerge automatically if slowly.

According to Mitrany (1975), all public action is political. As indicated above, functionalists expect their own kind of spillover but also expect contestation. What emerges is thus a certain principle of fostered gradualism, in which ideational change, and thus willingness to accept structural adaptation, are facilitated by deliberate agency and the creation of centripetal pressure by a 'vanguard' group of countries which takes part in a given sectoral organization. However, it should be noted that non-participation by a state in a given organization is not considered by functionalists to be problematic since their aim is not to create a new state or federation: providing the state participates in certain aspects of the system, as is likely in an economically interdependent world, there is no *a priori* difficulty (Hancock 1941–44).

Functionalism and Democracy
Unlike neofunctionalism, which sought to explain the development of a new federation in the absence of popular understanding let alone consent (Bellamy and Warleigh 1998), functionalism has solid democratic aspects and a more authentically cosmopolitan outlook—for example, Hancock (1941–44) maintained that the world network of agencies must grant citizenship to any individual who claimed it, rather than allow national governments to prevent the extension of such citizenship by refusing to participate in the global network.[9] Indeed, functionalists were among the first to notice the democratic deficit of the EU (Mitrany 1965), arguing that its attempts at state-building were an inadequate response to the emerging post-parliamentary mode of governance. Functionalists instead sought to reconfigure representative democracy along functional lines.

As noted above, functionalists considered that every agency should have a specialized assembly to which it would be held accountable. Representation would continue, but on an issue-specific basis rather than in the catch-all, aggregated fashion supposed to be the preserve of political parties in liberal democracies. Functionalists also laid emphasis on democracy of outcome. They argued that in a global network, as well as in modern national societies, it was idle to seek equality of participation for all since the necessary expertise is not held by

---

9.   However, it is not clear whether this would mean simply a generous common immigration régime or, far less likely, military action against such a recalcitrant state. Functionalist emphasis on spillover and avoidance of direct confrontation with national governments implies the former.

everyone to the same extent on any given issue. Instead, citizens as well as countries would delegate their individual rights to chosen representatives (much like in liberal democracy). The organization of politics on a functional basis would secure general equality of distribution, since there would be no territorially inspired motive to maximize the gain of one group over another for communitarian reasons (Mitrany 1975). Also, in common with liberal democracy, functionalists consider that individuals—and states—are free to enter into a multiplicity of overlapping relationships, which serve to ensure that power is not overly concentrated in the hands of any one actor/ group. Legitimacy is seen by functionalists to derive from administrative capacity and legislative output—that is, the maximization of welfare (Mitrany 1975). Again in contrast to neofunctionalism, Mitrany argues that it is not important to cultivate a sense of loyalty to the emerging order; this will emerge gradually and, in a functionalist context, will suffer far less from a backlash than the currently witnessed popular disquiet about the future progress of the EU.

As a result, functionalism has much in common with contemporary thinking about democracy beyond the nation state, which seeks to reconcile multiple identities while providing effective accountability of, and participation in, the process of international governance (see, *inter alia*, Curtin 1997; Chryssochoou 1998; Follesdal and Koslowski 1998; Lord 1998; and in particular, Jachtenfuchs, Diez and Jung 1998, who envisage a system of overlapping communities defined both territorially and functionally). In the next section of the chapter I set out a more detailed argument about the utility of functionalism in contemporary EU study.

The Return of Functionalism?

Why Rehabilitate Functionalism?
It is common to maintain that functionalism is a well-meaning, but naïve and technocratic approach to transnational governance which overemphasizes normative issues and simply misconstrues both human nature and the essence of international politics (O'Neill 1996: 33). Moreover, functionalists are often accused of ignoring the importance of politics and placing too much faith in rational processes of learning and socialization (Harrison 1975). The changes in popular attitude it sought have largely failed to materialize after roughly 50 years of

European integration (Blondel *et al.* 1998).[10] Functionalism can be elusive, responding weakly to such criticism by arguing that there has simply been an insufficient lapse of time for attitudes to alter significantly (Taylor 1975). Moreover, judged by the standards of mid to late twentieth-century social science, functionalism's status as a 'theory' is problematic: for example, its falsifiability is questionable (Taylor 1978b). Neofunctionalists, indeed, fundamentally altered the nature of their intellectual ancestor, aiming to increase its ability to explain political behaviour and change by adding a clearer account of agency and paying more attention to the dictates of social scientific rigour (Haas 1964). Given the failures of neofunctionalism and its attempted revival in the 1990s (Warleigh 1998), what possible reason could there be for returning to its predecessor?

The crucial factors here are as follows. First, as shown by a little intellectual archaeology, functionalism is simply not as unresponsive to the demands of 'proper' theory as is often claimed. Second, its differences from theories cast in that mould can be seen as advantageous rather than problematic. Third, functionalism provides a means of understanding the current state and likely future of European integration, both normatively and empirically, which is beyond the scope of other international relations-based theories. I deal with each of these aspects in turn.

How 'Scientific' Is Functionalism?

During the 1970s, scholars devoted much attention to functionalism as a serious alternative to neorealism and its emerging intergovernmentalist offspring. Pentland (1975) argued convincingly that functionalism can be considered more 'scientific' than is often assumed. Presaging the subsequent flight from Grand Theory, he argued that functionalism constitutes 'a promising middle way between the high road of model-building and the low road of pure induction' (Pentland 1975: 20).[11] It is possible to generate testable hypotheses about learning processes in international cooperation using functionalist principles; moreover, empirical testing of such hypotheses is eminently feasible. Function-

---

10. However, functionalists might reply that slow attitude change is in fact due to the confused nature of the EU—its mixture of functionalist and state-building aspects, which frustrates the 'natural' process of attitude change by placing that dynamic in a suffocating context of unwanted state-building.

11. The rest of this paragraph draws on Pentland 1975: 20-21.

alism's focus on output is commensurable with post-behaviouralist political science; its lack of fit with behaviouralism should not thus be equated with a lack of social scientific rigour. Moreover, functionalism urges scholars to focus on two issues which are of relevance to contemporary study. Its normative aspects are useful given the constant adaptation of the EU to changing circumstances, a trait in keeping with functionalism's prescription of gradual development based on response to a changing political-social-economic climate. Further, by sharing the usual international relations practice of training its perspective on all international agencies/organizations rather than single examples, functionalism sidesteps the 'N = 1' problem (the difficulty of trying to make generalizable theory about and based on a unique case study) which besets much contemporary EU theory (Rosamond 2000b).

Even sceptics might concede that functionalism has a clear value as a source of some description and eloquent prescription (Taylor 1975). Normatively, its emphasis on the development of consensus as the key agent of change is in keeping with much contemporary thinking on deliberative democracy and the EU (e.g. Eriksen and Fossum 2000). Moreover, it implies that successful integration (or at least transnationalization) can take place only as a result of gradual change in popular attitudes rather than élite social engineering (the neofunctionalist strategy). However, the bolder claim that functionalism has predictive and explanatory power might raise eyebrows. Nonetheless, a solid argument along these lines can be made, as shown by Taylor (1975), on whose work the following paragraph draws.

Despite its occasional lack of attention to detail (for example, there is little on precisely *how* form should follow function, in the language of the functionalist mantra), functionalism does offer the basis for making predictions about transnational governance. First, it argues that progress in deepening such arrangements will occur only when a supportive (popular) consensus can be generated. Second, it predicts that the 'constitutional' elements of transnational governance will need to evolve gradually over time rather then spring from a new kind of Philadelphia Convention. Third, it foresees that considerations of what is important in transnational governance will change over time and be affected by individual and group cooperation. In other words, it is not feasible to develop a detailed blueprint of how the dynamic process of integration should be reflected institutionally; its structures will have to evolve with it, locked in a two-way relationship as structure and agency/practice cause mutual evolution. The parallels with the contemporary EU are striking, and resound much more clearly than the visions offered by either neofunctionalist theory or state-centric scholarship given the Union's continuing location between international régime and new federation.

How Important Is 'Science'? The Costs of Orthodoxy
However, there are limits to the ability of functionalism to meet the requirements of contemporary political science in terms of qualifying as a 'theory'. According to Wilson-Green (1969: 61), Ernst Haas argued that Mitranian functionalism supplied an insufficient account of political behaviour. Moreover, such thought attempted to separate the inseparable on several scores. Haas (1968) disputed the functionalist arguments that power and welfare are discrete; that governance functions are separate, not inter-linked; that politicians and experts are necessarily different; and that loyalties are necessarily multiple. As a result, Haas held functionalist premises to be misconceived, and the resultant 'theory' unscientifically cast.[12] He also considered that functionalism relied too heavily on altruism as a catalyst; functionalism was too normative to develop a solid account of real-world political change (Haas 1968). In many ways sympathetic to functionalism—for example, it was considered by neofunctionalists to be both pragmatic and optimistic about the potential for transcending the nation state as a form of political organization—Haas nonetheless considered it unsuitable as a theory of what he and other neofunctionalists considered the new phenomenon called European integration. Highly underdetermined and culturally conditioned, functionalism was at best a usefully non-dogmatic, well-intentioned strategy for world peace, but one unsuitable for analysis of the presumed process of state-building in Europe since its chosen subject was different (Haas 1964).

Despite the arguments of Pentland and Taylor enlisted above, it is thus plain that functionalism's status as a scientifically sound 'theory' is debatable even if such criticisms are often overstated. What is less clear is the degree to which such a shortfall undermines functionalism's utility to scholars of the EU. It must be remembered that such a judgment propelled the entire neofunctionalist project to its demise, as

---

12. Incidentally, Wilson-Green disputes some of these arguments, claiming that the functionalist stress on institutions means Mitrany does in fact see a link between power and welfare.

the theory was largely abandoned in the 1970s thanks to its inability to meet its own rigorous demands (Haas 1975), before an unconvincing and brief partial resurrection twenty years later (Warleigh 1998). The history of 'integration theory' therefore reveals that the strictures of contemporary political science may not be a universal blessing: Haas and his followers set a standard which was impossible to meet, an event predicted by functionalists (Mitrany 1971). Functionalism's problematic status as a theory can thus be seen as a great advantage. Restricted falsifiability lends it a certain longevity denied other approaches whose paradigmatic assumptions must be rigid to be parsimonious. By focusing on issues rather than the development of a specific new form of governance to regulate them, functionalism ensures that scholars devote themselves to the promotion of solutions to problems rather than proselytize for a chosen new political structure, a weakness often attributed to neofunctionalism given its links with the community method of European integration (Harrison 1974).

Moreover, functionalists showed that contemporary political science should not take for granted the rightness of its chosen criteria or *Weltanschauung*. Mitrany (1971) challenged the parallel made between social and natural science, echoing the concerns of Kuhn himself about whether the two kinds of study are truly subject to commensurable methodologies and values (Kuhn 1970; 1977). Mitrany felt that the maelstrom of international politics rendered useless all attempts to construct detailed models of it. Too many real-life variables are screened out in the name of generating parsimonious theory. Moreover, in Mitranian thinking, political science fails in its main duty: replete with '(e)soteric constructions and idiosyncratic academic codes' (Mitrany 1971: 543), political science cannot show the way out of the cul-de-sac of political organization based on the concept of national sovereignty because it is too self-referential, responding to needs generated by gaps in theoretical constructs and false intellectual debates rather than real-world needs.[13]

---

13. Of course, this implies that political science *should* be relevant to the real world. But such an assumption is scarcely heretical, since even abstract work in political philosophy ultimately emanates from and relates back to attempts to generate a fairer (or at least better run) society. Consider, *inter alia*, Plato's *Republic* (written as a blueprint of the good society) or Machiavelli's *The Prince* (entirely conceived as a guide to the Medici family on how to govern Florence).

While such a judgment may not be entirely fair—there is no doubt that academic rigour in the contemporary sense helps generate well-grounded research—it is also clear that Mitrany's perspective is a convincing critique of the potentially stifling effect of overly determined and rigid 'theory'. Functionalism offers a depth of imagination and intellectual creativity which is screened out by more scientifically cast theories. Had the latter proved more successful, such a self-imposed limit would have mattered less. Given the shortcomings of orthodox integration theory, however, it represents a crucial weakness. Flexibility demonstrates the utility of an analytical framework such as functionalism which encourages the scholar to 'think outside the box', matching deductive and inductive reasoning in order to both expect and respond to change in the observed process/subject.

The Uses of Imagination: Functionalism and Flexibility

One of the major problems of neofunctionalism was its inability to sit well with flexibility, which has now become the principal logic of the Europolity.[14] Haas (1975: 83) argued that flexibility should be understood as the *failure* of integration, an indicator of incomplete *engrenage* and insufficient consensus-formation among the national élites. Although Haas (1975: 76-77) saw that different policy areas seemed to display different 'instrumentalities'—that is, institutional arrangements —he held this to reveal not just the problems of integration but also the impossibility of integration theory. Haas (1975: 79-85) prophetically envisaged a Europe of 'fragmented issue linkage' which defeated neofunctionalist theoretical endeavour. There would be no clear division of power between the EU and the national governments; no single planning system; no centrally coordinated information flow; no clear hierarchy; an evolving constitution; an *acquis* based on EU control of legislative intent rather than implementation—in short, a very different outcome from that sought by neofunctionalists, but one highly in keeping with both Mitranian thinking and current reality.[15] Monnet similarly—and rather illogically—considered such an outcome to the process he had deliberately started with the use of functionalist

14. See the next section of this chapter for an account of how flexibility is considered through non-neofunctionalist lenses.

15. Twenty-one years later, Philippe Schmitter (1996) returned to this line of thought in his model of the condominio, but even Schmitter omitted to give the model any normative (as opposed to explanatory/descriptive) value.

methods to be beyond the pale, a product of stagnation and intergovernmental intransigence rather than the probable outcome of his attempt
to build a federal state by stealth (Monnet 1978: 479).[16]

Curtin (1995) offers a typical contemporary account of flexibility.
Admitting the long history of the phenomenon in the tale of European
integration, Curtin nonetheless argues that flexibility should be understood as an attack on the developing European constitutional order,
given the fact that recent opt-outs have been granted as a result of
deliberate political choice rather than inability to meet socio-economic
criteria (e.g. UK and Danish opt-outs from the single currency). In a
thoughtful piece, Curtin grants that a kind of two-speed Europe might
be permissible if a hard core of policy areas were determined and
formed a non-negotiable obligation of EU membership, and provides a
sensible blueprint for how this arrangement might work (Curtin 1995:
250-51). Nonetheless, there is a clear warning that flexibility is incompatible with constitutionalization, and thus state/polity-building, in
Europe. From Curtin's perspective, this is self-evidently a bad thing.[17]
Many other scholars are similarly cautious about flexibility. Ehlermann
(1984) argues that the way in which EC law is constructed—the use of
directives (which grant member governments ample room regarding
implementation) as well as entirely binding regulations, in addition to
the important role of national courts in the EU legal system—obviates
the need for political flexibility, whose existence is therefore puzzling.
Several other scholars maintain that the use of flexibility to date reveals
the lack of a guiding normative basis; the Treaty reflects different kinds
of flexibility (Chaltiel 1998), an insufficient set of organizing principles

---

16. Intriguingly, such absolutist and limited thinking blinded Monnet to the
utility of opting-out. According to Monnet's memoirs, de Gaulle was offered the
Luxembourg Compromise—the retention of the national veto—as a means of
bringing France back into the fold after its refusal to countenance CAP reform and
an increase in the powers of the then European Assembly. Had he instead been
offered use of an opt-out clause, the history of integration might have been very
different. Similarly, Monnet's insistence that the UK must have full membership of
the (then) EEC or nothing contributed to the delay in British accession to the Union;
a kind of association agreement might have satisfied the British in the short term
while allowing de Gaulle to feel the Americans' Trojan horse tactics could be
frustrated.

17. Although other legal scholars disagree; see MacCormick 1993; Tuytschaever
1999 and the collected essays in De Búrca and Scott 2000.

and an uneasy mixture of managerialism and implicit, only partially formed, ideological choices (Shaw 1998).

Consequently, flexibility is academically controversial even though certain member states appear to be seeking to create a vanguard group and deepen their mutual integration.[18] Such caution is, to some extent, laudable: scholars are right to question the different strategies for flexibility put forward by member states and assess their relative strengths and weaknesses. They are also right to point out and analyse the contradictions of an EU struggling with a process of constant reform and both centripetal and centrifugal pressures. However, it is tempting to see such contradictions as somehow necessarily suboptimal, and this is not necessarily the case: such judgments tend to be based on paradigmatic, and thus normative, assumptions based on either models of the (federal) state—in which case the EU is insufficiently integrated and too disparate for even federalism safely to encompass—or the international régime—in which case, the EU is far too integrated for normative well-being. A more imaginative response is to embrace the conceptual middle ground in which flexibility is the key to the development of the EU as a system of transnational governance, since it allows the articulation of difference and seeks not a uniform model but rather different and evolving patterns of integration according to felt need. In this light, functionalism enjoys analytical value as both explanatory device—it shows how integration can begin and then progress as a process of joint problem resolution—and as a normative framework, in which European integration is viewed as a strategy for cooperation and security, with regional polity-building a by-product and step on the way to a global system rather than the ultimate goal of the process. It is now appropriate to return to the issue of flexibility in order to establish more certainly the ability of both functionalism and various state-centric theories of transnational governance in Europe to explain and provide a normative basis for this central dynamic of contemporary integration.[19]

18. Witness German and French plans for further flexibility, currently debated as part of the 'post-Nice' process.

19. The problems caused to neofunctionalism by the phenomenon of flexibility were discussed above.

Intergovernmentalism, Consociationalism and Flexibility: The Case of 'Closer Cooperation'

State-centric Theories and Flexibility

Explaining why a given member state might seek to use flexibility as a means of deepening integration is not a problem in state-centric integration theory—it can be considered as pursuit of the 'national interest' in keeping with any other decision to commit to, or continue, European integration (Moravcsik 1993; 1999). Flexibility is thus really about the establishment of a core Europe, a *directoire* in which the heavyweight member states develop a joint hegemony. Likewise, it is easy to explain why a member state might oppose flexibility from this perspective: it would not wish to allow other member states to take the integration process towards goals which it does not support, and would thus use its veto power to prevent such an outcome. The central problem in state-centric accounts of flexibility is thus how to explain the decision of all member governments to allow a vanguard group of their fellows to establish itself within the confines of the Treaty, even on a case-by-case basis. This is because it signals the deliberate eradication of the culture of consensus which has been such a feature of the workings of the Council to date (Sherrington 2000: 164-65).

At first sight, this may seem counter-intuitive. After all, what could be greater proof of continued national sovereignty than its use to opt out of an unwanted policy régime?

However, intergovernmentalist theory holds as its baseline that states are jealous of their power, and will not agree to the *de facto* stripping of their sovereignty without the very kind of gain or major side-payment which flexibility does not give: non-participant states merely avoid whatever costs are involved with the given initiative and fail to reap the greater part of the gains. To a certain extent, there may be a potential for 'free riding': for example, if the Euroland economies grow as well as forecast, the UK will benefit to a degree through its participation in the single market, even if it will lose the ability to shape vital decisions in the governance of the currency regime. There may be substantial domestic or international pressures which would make participation difficult, for example Irish non-participation in the Schengen process followed logically from the UK opt-out. In general, however, a member government which opposes a new measure being brought into Treaty competence, or the extension of Community power in a given policy area, should seek to restrain its partners. It should ensure as a first-string strategy that it is possible to veto any such attempt, since a suitable package deal/bargain is unlikely. Failing that, it should insist that all member states, not just those which participate in the flexibility scheme, should be able to decide by unanimity what the pioneer group does. Should this not be possible, a member government should at least insist on recourse to qualified majority voting (QMV) by all member states rather than just the participants, so that it can seek to create a blocking minority if necessary. Otherwise, the central logic of intergovernmentalist theory is brought into question.

Consociation theorists have similar problems in analysing flexibility. By explaining integration outcomes as the result of a search for consensus between member governments of ostensible equality, scholars like Taylor (1993; 1996; 1997) and Chryssochoou (1994; 1997) place considerable emphasis on the drive for unanimity which they perceive member states to privilege. The EU makes decisions because, through package deals and side-payments, all member governments reach an agreement, at least on first-order issues such as Treaty change where unanimous voting remains. Qualified majority voting is a red herring; it exists more as a threat than a reality, and its provisions are rarely used. Consequently, flexibility is more illusion than reality: by menacing recalcitrant partners with the prospect of being left behind, those with a strong line on an issue can perhaps 'persuade' others to fall into line (Taylor 1996). By quietly continuing supposedly temporary derogations, both individual member states and, in the case of conditions placed on new states' accession, the existing members as a collective, can use this mechanism as a means of expressing the collective will (de la Serre and Wallace 1997). Nonetheless, it is impossible to square the search for consensus with the open abandoning of uniformity as a style of governance/integration. At best, it could serve to explain the drive for élite deliberation within each sub-cabal of the EU. As an explanation of the general pattern of integration, however, it fails completely: unanimity is one of the few things in political life which is truly indivisible by definition. However, it is necessary to assess whether state-centric theories possess any greater explanatory power concerning the specific model of closer cooperation than they enjoy vis-à-vis flexibility in general.

State-centric Theory and 'Closer Cooperation'

State-centric scholars view the Amsterdam Treaty provisions on closer cooperation as evidence that member states control the issue of flexibility and are reluctant to see its use as a radical new basis for EU governance. As Chryssochoou *et al.* (1999) demonstrate, the principle of flexibility certainly shows that the member states are now engaged in a process of polity-building rather than traditional intergovernmental diplomacy because they are using it to tackle issues which undoubtedly deepen the integration process, such as the single currency. However, they emphasize that closer cooperation is not being used to unblock other key policy areas in which progress has long been difficult (e.g. the CFSP, whose Amsterdam provisions on 'constructive abstention' are read as cautious, and where the national veto remains even after Nice[20]). Closer cooperation is thus best considered a necessary and pragmatic response to three key factors (existing opt-outs; certain member states' inability/lack of desire to join the euro; and the prospect of further enlargement) which allowed member governments to reassert control over the integration process (Chryssochoou *et al.* 1999).[21]

It is perhaps Thomas Pedersen, however, who provides the most subtle intergovernmentalist account of closer cooperation (CC). In a thoughtful article (Pedersen 2000), he argues that CC is best seen as a strategic device to enable the emergence over time of a vanguard group of member states, in which a strategy of 'federal asymmetry' is pursued in order to force laggard states to catch up after appreciating the costs of non-involvement. This is a difficult manoeuvre, involving a balancing act of some complexity since non-participants must not be alienated by the pioneers (and, as discussed above, they must agree to the establishment of the vanguard group in the first place). Flexibility is presented as an alternative to exit threats by the major EU powers: 'small states' accept flexibility given their dependence on the 'Big Three', and only the absence of the UK from the likely vanguard prevents Germany and France from establishing a *directoire*. Given the

20. It is true, however, that 'constructive abstention' co-existed with, and helped shape the supportive environment for, the development of the Rapid Reaction Force, implying that even in matters of the CFSP this judgment is open to review.

21. However, it must be remembered that the role of the Court of Justice is important. By 'communitarizing' Schengen, member governments gave the accords the full force of EC law (Shaw 1998), to which even the UK is now bending its will through a slow process of unofficial opting-in.

UK's position, Germany and France are obliged to establish (and then revise) a CC-like scheme in which the consociational culture is being undermined even with regard to 'constitutional policy' (Pedersen 2000: 211), given the shift away from formal equality of national systems in terms of Treaty ratification. As a result, Pedersen expects enlargement to provide the justification for increased recourse to flexibility—CC is the first explicit attempt to insert the principle into the Treaty, and one which will be revisited, as 'performance-oriented and sovereignty-conscious state executives in the big member states look for new forms of supranationality on the cheap' (Pedersen 2000: 211).

Much was read by other intergovernmentalists into the claimed first formal recognition of the 'Luxembourg Compromise', the Amsterdam Treaty clauses relating to CC, in which member governments were allowed to veto attempts to trigger CC operations by citing reasons of vital and stated national policy (Devuyst 1998, 1999; Moravcsik and Nicolaidis 1999). Thus, CC should be read as part of a clear strategy by the major member governments to ensure a minimal role for the non-Council institutions in policy making (Devuyst 1999), in which the rise of soft law and challenges to the authority of the Commission and the Court of Justice sit alongside the use of flexibility rather than agreement significantly to extend—and use—QMV. Moreover, the Amsterdam negotiations revealed a more complex, if still sovereignty-conscious, kind of multi-level intergovernmentalism, with the assertion of Euro-scepticism by the German *Land* governments which had to be taken into account by German negotiators (Devuyst 1998).

Thus, intergovernmentalists can also convincingly explain why unanimity is required to allow flexibility to add to the *acquis* via Treaty change.

Even before the changes wrought by the Nice Treaty, however, intergovernmentalist explanation of closer cooperation was not entirely convincing. The informal 'gentlemen's agreement' (*sic*) constituted by the original Luxembourg Compromise potentially blocked all legislation; the Amsterdam veto clause applies only to measures proposed for CC, a quantitative difference which is also qualitative given the continuing debate about the permissible scope of flexibility (Junge 1999). As demonstrated by Philippart and Sie Dian Ho (2000), the Amsterdam Treaty version of flexibility contained not just intergovernmental elements, but also functional/regulatory and multi-level governance aspects, based on the ability to allow deepening according to functional need and a limited revisiting of the subsidiarity principle, although in their view it is the intergovernmental and functional elements which are more evident. After Nice, the national veto remains only in pillar 2, and even here the feasibility of closer cooperation was enhanced by the new Treaty. The clumsiness of the Amsterdam triggering mechanism was such that CC was unlikely to be enacted and thus prevent the frustration of member governments seeking deeper integration, in turn making either further Treaty change or extra-Treaty cooperation likely. Thus, as signalled by Pedersen, CC *à la* Amsterdam was always likely to be only a holding strategy rather than a definitive conclusion of the debate. The victory of the reluctant member states in imposing such strict launching criteria contradicted what would be considered their key objective from a mainstream intergovernmentalist viewpoint (namely the containment of the integrationist desires of their peers in the absence of a major side-payment or alternative bargain), and was thus entirely Pyrrhic.

As a result, while CC clearly contains facets in keeping with intergovernmentalist thought, it is unlikely that even the Nice variant is the definitive interpretation of the flexibility principle—as shown by its centrality in Franco-German plans for the subsequent stage of EU reform. To understand flexibility in its entirety, therefore, we need to use a different and less state-centric conceptual lens. In terms of explanatory power, intergovernmentalism is less useful than claims based on the supposed Treaty recognition of the Luxembourg Compromise, or the argument that CC is a veil to hide *de facto* containment of the likely pioneer group by the laggard states, suggest. More convincing is the claim that CC represents the first step towards the establishment of a *directoire*. However, the likely continued resistance of the UK to such a development detracts from this view; without its inclusion, Franco-German cooperation cannot create such a joint hegemony across the board, only in specific policy fields. Instead, given the general wish in the national capitals to avoid relegation to a clear second-tier status, Franco-German plans are more likely to result in a system of overlapping cores in which membership alters according to the policy area. It must be remembered that all Treaty change is ultimately the product of intergovernmental agreement, and is thus likely to produce a functionally defined and differentiated Europolity.

Conclusions: Theorizing Flexibility—The Uses of Functionalism

A Flexible Europe: The Functionalist View

It is helpful at this stage briefly to summarize the central arguments of functionalism. When Haas (1975) rejected neofunctionalism, he predicted that the EU would develop on the basis of 'asymmetrical overlap' in which 'several authoritative institutions co-exist with ill-demarcated boundaries between them—each with primary responsibility for some item in the package of linked issues' (Haas 1975: 84-85). The parallels with today's Europe, in which the increasingly differentiated EU is but one of several organizations involved with the governance of the continent, are striking. Within the EU, flexibility has added to the traditional coexistence of variegated policy regimes, vindicating Haas's prediction. Most theoretical approaches consider this situation problematic or in some way suboptimal. Functionalism, on the other hand, sees it as a normative good, the kind of arrangement most likely to guarantee security on the continent.

It will be recalled that functionalists advocate a pattern of differentiated governance regimes in which rational decisions about the most efficient way to carry out their respective public tasks dictates the political structure. Countries with particular expertise in a given area could be allowed to take the lead in the name of the particular agency, within the limit that their actions should be in the general interest (Mitrany 1944: 34) and accountable to functional (i.e. sector-specific) parliaments. In the evolving system of governance sought by functionalists, a premium is placed on the coexistence of various functional agencies whose powers would not be identical, but rather dictated by the needs appropriate to a given policy area.

Functionalism allows the recognition of differences between states in terms of power. However, it seeks to reduce the capacity of these differences to cause conflict by harnessing states to multiple lattice-works of transnational, functional cooperation in which differences of both power and interest matter less. Functionalists even go so far as to allow opting-out; states with no inclination to participate in a given agency are free to stay out of it (Mitrany 1944; Hancock 1941–44). Coordination between the various agencies should be left to develop organically, with the erection of no over-arching political authority: instead of replicating the state, functionalists call for a complex set of structures which may preserve the edifice of the nation-state while altering its *modus operandi*. Functional arrangements are open-ended: they can survive secession, enlargement and bilateral cooperation between their members and non-members. They can survive such activity without damage to either their workings or their underlying rationale (Mitrany 1944: 43). Finally, functionalism offers states a kind of supranationalism which poses a less overt challenge to their sovereignty: states which balk at transfer of power to a single state-in-waiting may feel less threatened by a more disparate range of sector-specific agencies.

The CC provisions of the Treaty offer many links with functionalist thinking. Institutionalized differentiation has been part of the EU process since Maastricht, and functional differentiation was inherited from the ECSC. Although he concludes that the intergovernmentalist account is more convincing since leading member states will seek to use flexibility as a means of imposing their agenda, and since extra-EU cooperation by member states is at least partly delegitimized by the inclusion of CC in the Treaty, Pedersen (2000: 211) argues that functionalism is evident in the way CC has developed, reflecting the Union's emphasis on incrementalism, segmentation and deconstitutionalization. Wessels (1998) argues that Amsterdam saw member governments abandon the idea of a common end goal for the integration process, seeking instead a more pick-and-mix approach while avoiding the total freedom of the *à la* carte model. Such a view shows partial reflection of functionalist thinking, although functionalists would arguably prefer the absence of political constraints on the freedom of member states to select their own respective destinations from within the range of possible outcomes to the integration process. The reforms made to CC at Nice also point towards functionalist outcomes from intergovernmental decisions, through the abolition of the national veto in pillars 1 and 3 and the facilitation of the emergence of regime-specific sub-groups of member states (by the abolition of the requirement that such regimes must involve a majority of member states). Additionally, the continuing managerial approach to closer cooperation is inherently functionalist.

The constitutional impact of the CC provisions is still unclear. For some observers, flexibility in its Amsterdam guise was managerial rather than a device for radical polity-building, a deliberate and deplorable attempt to avoid the difficult ideological choices to be made concerning the development of the Europolity (Shaw 1998). For others, it provided the basis for further reform predicated on grounds of efficiency and the need to avoid post-enlargement stagnation (Von Weizsäcker, Dehaene and Simon 1999)—which is what the Nice Treaty produced. Whatever view one takes on this issue, it is clear that closer cooperation denotes the EU's departure from the orthodox Community Method in a direction which has normative as well as technocratic connections with functionalism. It remains to explore the uses of functionalism as a working theory of European governance.

A Working Theory of European Governance?
Earlier in this chapter, I argued that functionalism's use as a theory of European governance could be clarified on three counts. First, its differences from the demands of 'proper' theory are less drastic than is often claimed. Second, its differences from theories cast in that mould can be seen as advantageous rather than problematic. Third, function-alism provides a means of understanding the current condition and likely future of European integration both normatively and empirically, an achievement which is beyond the scope of other international relations-based theories. The latter is an especially important benefit given the inability of comparative politics approaches, increasingly and logically used to study the public policy making of the Union, to provide that normative base, since such is not their concern. At this stage of the chapter it is appropriate to consider further issues in order to establish functionalism's continuing pertinence to a specifically regional rather than global undertaking.

First, it must be acknowledged that the functionalist's view of the EU is likely to be at best ambivalent. Although it is not impossible to reconcile the global perspective of the functionalists with regional enterprises like the Union if the latter remains open to, and a participant in, international functional arrangements (Wilson-Green 1969), and functionalists did foresee that functional cooperation could result in a (global) federation, there are several points to bear in mind. Given the highly normative nature of functionalism, these reservations are all the more important since they reflect a solid conception of what the EU could and should become. Mitrany thought that progress in public life must come through depoliticization—the transformation of political issues into social/welfare concerns, since he saw politics as inevitably divisive. He had grave doubts as to whether such changes could be achieved successfully on a regional scale, since regional integration replicated the structures of the nation state too strongly. This would cause two major problems: greater reluctance on the part of member states to pool their sovereignty (since they would fear abnegation in a new overarching state), and the likelihood that, if successful, regional integration would simply recreate the dangers of nationalism on a broader scale (Mitrany 1975). Acceptable as features of a devolved global system, regional blocs are, for functionalists, otherwise to be avoided. However, an evolving entity like the EU is only partially akin to the kind of regional bloc mistrusted by functionalists: for instance, it still has an evolving 'constitution', and periodically takes in further members. Moreover, in the emerging European order, the EU is currently only one of several agencies at work in European governance, albeit by far the most successful and with the broadest remit. These factors allow the application of functionalist theory to the EU, albeit with the rider that the Union must not become a solipsistic federation in its own right.

Secondly, there may be doubts regarding the coherence of functionalism in a global political economy in which nation states are increasingly unimportant, since functionalists placed a great deal of emphasis on the planned or at least heavily regulated economy typical of the early welfare state (Rosamond 2000a). However, interdependent economies arguably facilitate functional integration; and if the latter is interpreted as an attempt to exercise as much sovereignty as possible (Milward 1994), then functionally based attempts to counter the influence of global business will appeal to all but the most devoted neo-liberal, even if they do not replicate the welfare structures of the nation state (Scharpf 1999).

Thirdly, functionalism places too great an emphasis on what it considers 'rational activity' without accepting that different paradigms dictate diverging considerations of what this comprises (Rosamond 2000a). Clearly, persuasion must be possible or else there is no future for political debate. However, functionalists need to pay greater attention to the idea of cognitive change since they place such stress on attitudinal transformation as the baseline of integration. Undertaking this adaptation would help alleviate a further problem, namely the lack of specificity in the theory concerning how form should follow function. Mitrany held that it was idle to set out a blueprint since politics is about evolution and context, a powerful argument even today. However, as a guide for reform which lays such a stress on normative judgments, functionalists could usefully develop a more detailed, or at least updated, blueprint of the EU and world governance than those developed by Mitrany (1933; 1944) and Hancock (1941–44).

The above reservations should be interpreted as the outlines of a research agenda rather than immovable barriers to the use of functionalism in EU study. Functionalism is far from the naïve and apolitical approach of caricature; it is instead an open-ended theory of how to secure peace through cooperation in international agencies of collective governance. It can help scholars and practitioners recast their notions of what the EU can or should achieve, and help reorient study of the EU as part of the current 'normative turn'. Flexibility, including its closer cooperation variant, demonstrates the beginnings of rapprochement between the EU and both the normative and the empirical aspects of functionalist theory, but this process is far from complete. In the next chapter I therefore examine the ongoing elaboration of flexibility as it continues its evolution.

3 |

'Closer Cooperation': Flexibility from Amsterdam to Nice

Introduction

Although the advent of flexibility came much earlier in the integration progress, it was during the 1990s that the first real attempts were made to elaborate it as an explicit principle of Union governance. In the Maastricht Treaty, the three pillar system was established, and European integration was officially and explicitly opened up to differentiation (Duff 1997a). However, the Maastricht Treaty did not set out any rules for the use of flexibility as a tool for day-to-day policy making. In this Treaty, flexibility appears as a choice only for 'history-making' decisions (Peterson 1995), that is, for matters related to the agreement of new Treaties. 'Europhoria' was at its height: many thought that the EU would become federalized very shortly afterwards as a result of the momentum raised by the completion of the single market (itself mostly in place by 1 January 1993), the launch of the euro (for which a timetable and entrance criteria were set out in the Maastricht Treaty), and the collapse of the communist regimes in Central and Eastern Europe, which cleared the path to enlargement across the continent (Wistrich 1991). It is only with hindsight that the extent to which such judgments were illusory has been made clear. Instead of smooth progress towards 'ever closer union', the 1990s produced contested and limited further developments as member governments sought above all to keep the launch of EMU on track, while wrestling with the still unresolved major issues of institutional reform (Devuyst 1998).

Thus, it was left to the Treaties of Amsterdam and Nice to set out the actual workings of flexibility—or 'closer cooperation', as it is called in the treaty. Coming later in the decade than Maastricht, they were shaped by the existing climate of caution and also by the increasing and often critical debate about the role of the EU at both public and elite levels. Neither Amsterdam nor Nice were as ambitious as Maastricht; although they added to the latter's achievements, the net increase in the level and scope of integration via the two latest treaties was less than that achieved by Maastricht, although of course certain important steps were thereby taken (such as the extension and simplification of codecision at Amsterdam and the agreement about the weighting of votes in Council at Nice). However, the primary achievement of the Amsterdam and Nice treaties was to first introduce and then facilitate flexibility as a principle and practice of day-to-day EU governance, thereby potentially allowing it to colour the entire integration process. Thus, this chapter focuses on closer cooperation and its evolving elaboration.

Closer Cooperation and the Amsterdam Treaty

The Treaty of Amsterdam (ToA) is an essential document in the history of the EU if for no other reason than its 'constitutionalization' of CC (Shaw 2000) in Articles 5a, K12 and K15–17. By establishing an initial set of rules for the use of flexibility as a tool of decision making, the ToA was highly innovative. Moreover, it also thereby added a challenge to the orthodox perspective of legal integration since it pushed the Union towards 'open-ended...constitutional politics' (Shaw 2000: 339) rather than the traditional view that EC law could and should be a tool for deepening integration by its erection of a uniform, entirely binding and wholly supreme legal order (see Chapter 4).

In fact, the ToA ensured that flexibility (as CC) could be applied in two different ways—first, as opt-outs from entire policy areas (as had been established at Maastricht); second, as opt-outs from particular measures within a policy area, even when a member state did not oppose many, or indeed any, of the other measures in that area. As an example of this kind of CC, pillar 2 was given the practice of 'constructive abstention', according to which member states opposed to a particular proposal in CFSP could abstain rather than veto and thereby allow other member states to proceed with their plans to cooperate.

However, CC was clearly presented in the ToA in a manner which did as little as possible to make its normative implications clear:

although it provided further clarification of how flexibility was to function as a key feature of Union governance, it was presented as a managerial rather than an ideological principle, and clear indications of its scope were not made (Shaw 1998). Thus, it was a fairly limited application of the flexibility principle. Duff (1997b: 186-87) argues that it was agreed almost entirely as a response to UK intransigence on a whole range of issues, from matters of genuine difference about policy (e.g. EMU) to multiple battles over BSE, fish quotas and social policy, a view supported by Tuytschaever (1999).

The ToA produced a form of CC which allowed flexibility to be applied in pillars 1 and 3, and an equivalent ('constructive abstention') to be deployed in pillar 2. It also gave the power to decide whether and when member states initially outside a CC measure could subsequently join it to the Commission (rather than the Council)—at least in pillar 1. In pillars 2 and 3, the Council retained more power, both to propose and to decide on the subsequent ability to join of those member states which initially opt out. Even in pillar 1, however, the Treaty also allowed member states to veto the launch of a CC measure for 'important and stated reasons of national policy' (Article 5a(2)). Thus, even though CC was agreed, it was arguably possible for any member state to prevent its use. Should a CC measure be launched, it would work under the same decision rules as if it had been a whole-EU measure (i.e. consultation, cooperation, assent or codecision, according as always to the legal base) (Kortenberg 1998). Thus, although they had no say over the launch of CC, in pillar 1 the EP and the ECJ were empowered by Amsterdam to play the same role in decision making in CC measures once they had been set in train as they would otherwise have done. Within the Council, only participating member states retained the right to vote on a CC measure. The Commission, as stated above, retained a key role in pillar 1, and was also empowered in pillar 3 (although the ECJ and EP were not).

The budget would be paid by participating member states, unless the Council agreed unanimously that all member states would pay out of the EU budget (Chaltiel 1998). The launch of CC would be by QMV, provided that no member state vetoed it. If a member state used its veto power to block the launch, no vote would be taken, and the proposal would fall—if, that is, the member state in question stated reasons that the other national governments were prepared to accept as worthy. In the case of doubts on this issue, the ToA provided for a sort of 'trial by peers' of the recalcitrant member state—it could be called to defend its reasoning to the European Council. Thus, it was not clear whether a veto over the launch of CC was in fact absolute—and this was never put to the test since the ToA was only brought into force in 1999 after a slow ratification process, and 2000 saw the agreement of the Treaty of Nice revisions.[1] Similarly, there was no clear ruling about the necessary number of participants in a CC measure. Although CC would be launched by QMV, and therefore would require the agreement of roughly two-thirds of the weighted votes of the member states, it would require only a 'majority' of member states to actually want to participate, leaving unclear the issue of how many member states would constitute a quorum (Kortenberg 1998).

Finally, the ToA added several limits to the application of closer cooperation. It stated explicitly that CC could not be used to add new areas of policy competence to the EU—instead, it could only be used to allow further legislation to be built up in areas where the EU had already been granted authority to act. Similarly, it was not allowed to undermine EU citizenship. Thus, while the Treaty had already allowed flexibility to be applied to the addition of new EU competence by the member states at an intergovernmental summit (e.g. EMU), closer cooperation was explicitly prevented from fulfilling the same function. In addition, it added that the *acquis communautaire* could not be unpicked by CC, and that the institutional framework of the Union must be preserved (i.e. no new institutions could be created to allow the management of CC measures by participating member states). Furthermore, it ruled that CC should be an issue of last resort rather than an everyday occurrence, and that those member states which initially opt out must have the ability to opt in subsequently (Junge 1999; Philippart and Edwards 1999).

Thus, the ToA left many unresolved issues regarding CC even while it built on the lead given by Maastricht. First, it was regarded by many observers as rather timid and underdeveloped, and therefore likely to frustrate those member states which had sought to use it as a means of deepening integration (Scharpf 1999). It lacked clarity on several counts, such as the lack of specificity about which policy areas it was applicable to (Shaw 1998). Moreover, it was possessed of a very

1.   At the time of writing, the Nice Treaty has yet to be ratified. It is thus possible that the ToA provisions for flexibility will be used in anticipation of the new Treaty.

clumsy triggering mechanism which provided both the Commission and the member states with veto powers in the first pillar, and gave similar blocking powers to the member states in pillars 2 and 3. Thus, it was not clear whether CC was actually capable of operation. It also left unsettled issues of subsidiarity and the right to extra-EU cooperation by member states, which it may have delegitimized but did not preclude (Gaja 1998). It was unclear whether 'constructive abstention' would be sufficient to allow progress in pillar 2, and thus whether a more adventurous kind of flexibility would be needed also in CFSP matters (Philippart and Edwards 1999). There were additional doubts concerning the interinstitutional balance, as the EP resented its exclusion from both the launching mechanism for CC and its operation in pillar 3.

The existence of these problems requires explanation.[2] Although the purposes of the member states can be served by ambiguity in the Treaty, as was notoriously the case with subsidiarity (Peterson 1994), it is far from clear that such an agreement as that in the ToA about closer cooperation was intended by all the relevant actors to be definitive. There are two main ways of explaining the compromise which shaped the ToA outcome on CC: as deliberate intergovernmental strategy; and as unfinished business, itself resulting from poor or at least incomplete negotiation.

The first approach draws on the general trend towards slowing down the pace of integration over the 1990s and the attendant shift away from 'hard' legislation to various kinds of soft policy (see Wallace 2000b for a summary of the latter). It emphasizes the existence of the member states' veto power in the trigger mechanism, and argues that CC shows the Union to be the victim of its own success: as the EU becomes empowered in more and more policy areas, it is less subject to control by national foreign ministries and more susceptible to both domestic party politics and the inclinations of national ministries with other portfolios. In turn, both the latter are in general less 'Europeanized' than the foreign ministries, which have become used to working with and through the EU over time (Devuyst 1999). Additionally, the ToA revealed that the member states were seeking to reduce the powers of the Commission (see Cini 2001), and even to become their own agents of policy to a greater extent (Moravcsik and Nicolaidis 1999).

2.   The theoretical implications of this are discussed in Chapter 2.

The second approach emphasizes the process of negotiation which led to the ToA itself. Devuyst (1998) notes that the Reflection Group which prepared the Amsterdam Summit was not in general composed of heavyweight figures empowered to negotiate solutions to problems, a role which the heads of state and government kept to themselves. Thus, it was unable to present the summit with a set of clear and thorough recommendations which had already eliminated several key differences of opinion between the member states. While this point is entirely in keeping with intergovernmental explanations—the latter would postulate that even during the preparatory stage member states were keen to limit the possibilities for radical reform of the Union—it also has links with the comments of those inclined to privilege procedural concerns. Stubb (2000) argues that the election of a new and less obviously obstructionist British government halfway through preparations for the summit lessened the degree of urgency attached to the issue of flexibility by those who had seen it as a means of avoiding British intransigence. Instead, flexibility was seen primarily as an institutional issue rather than one of principle or ideology, and issues such as 'what flexibility was really needed for, whom it would benefit or in which areas it would operate' were deliberately left for the future to resolve (Stubb 2000: 170).

Helen Wallace (2000a) similarly notes that negotiations about flexibility had become more complicated since Maastricht for various important reasons. The third and final stage of EMU was imminent, meaning that a major case study of the institutional issues related to flexibility would soon be at hand—it might thus be more sensible to wait in order to maximize learning potential. Second, the 1995 enlargement of the Union to Sweden, Finland and Austria had increased the number of member states which were able to meet the criteria for joining in policy already subject to flexibility, but whose will to do so could not be taken for granted, thus making it clear that flexibility had (and has) political and normative rather than merely organizational implications. Third, there were the beginnings of the elision of economic and military integration—although the latter remains fledgling and was largely dictated by extra-EU cooperation (in particular the Franco-British St Malo initiative), it has so far produced the Rapid Reaction Force and may yet deepen the CFSP further. Thus, it became clear that the potential for flexibility as a means of deepening integration remained, and also that there was interplay between extra- and intra-EU cooperation. In other words, flexibility was potentially a highly useful tool, but not necessarily one which should remain entirely within the Treaty structure, and whose regulation within the Treaty should thus itself be flexible. The upcoming enlargement to many countries of Central and Eastern Europe, however, meant that flexibility remained on the agenda of the IGC, since there was general agreement that internal diversity would thereby increase, and thus some kind of systematization of flexibility should begin. Finally, immigration issues, introduced firmly into EU competence by Maastricht, were rising up the agenda, and again pointed towards an aspect of cooperation which most member states considered suitable for action at EU level—hence the incorporation of the Schengen accords on freedom of movement. Thus the ToA outcome on CC is a product of how the negotiations were handled as a result of both actor choices and historical context (Kortenberg 1998).

Of course, the two explanations are not irreconcilable, since Treaty reform has to date been a matter of intergovernmental decision making, albeit with the ability of other actors (the Commission; interest groups; third states; the EP) to influence some decisions to a limited degree (Closa 1998). Both point towards the limited outcome of the ToA and the changing methods by which European integration is carried out. Nonetheless, what emerges from the first explanation is an idea of deliberate and predetermined member state choice: CC is ultimately about enshrining the member states' veto power, and thus reflects a compromise between the wishes of Germany and France (to promote flexibility) and the wishes of the UK (to frustrate flexibility as far as possible). What emerges from the second explanation is a more contingent analysis, dependent on context and actors. The principal difference is that the second view is less deterministic, and less likely to consider the ToA outcome as typical of the likely end-point.

From Amsterdam to Nice: Revisiting Closer Cooperation

In this respect it is interesting that the Treaty of Nice (ToN) did make certain significant changes to the configuration of CC, and thus built on the foundations laid at Amsterdam. Clearly, the member states were not entirely satisfied with the tool they had forged for themselves in the ToA. In essence this was because it was not sufficiently clear that the benefits sought by proponents of flexibility could actually be ensured by CC in its Amsterdam guise: although the Treaty stated that CC could only be used to deepen integration and not to unpick the *acquis*, it was not clear that the agreement made at Amsterdam was really workable. It was certainly never put to the test.

Concerns were focused on the following issues. First, the rather clumsy and difficult process of triggering was identified as a weakness; institutionally, CC was considered to add complexity to the EU's structures without bringing any certain benefits (Ehlermann 1998). Second, CC was confused and under-specified; de la Serre and Wallace 1997) point out that even after Amsterdam, EMU remained the only policy area with explicit criteria for the application of flexibility and clear links to the rest of the Union institutional system. There were concerns about the extension of the 'democratic deficit' to flexibility given the EP's lack of ability to decide about the launching of a CC measure even if it had codecision rights over any subsequent legislation. EC lawyers noted that the CC provisions did nothing to prevent member states launching extra-EU cooperation, either as a first choice strategy or if they failed to get sufficient support for their proposals to collaborate under the CC provisions (Tuytschaever 1999; De Witte 2000). Thus, CC was in danger of not achieving one of flexibility's key advantages from the perspective of those who saw it as a means of deepening the integration process. Moreover, the ToA was also ambiguous on the issues of power and responsibility; while member states participating in CC would have to abide by EU practices and use its institutions, it was a moot point whether only the sub-group of these states or the EU as a whole would be credited with competence in policies enacted under CC (Tuytschaever 1999). Thus, both politically and legally there were key issues to be resolved. Indeed, reforming closer cooperation became a key issue by the time of the ToN in order to prepare for enlargement to Central and Eastern Europe and ensure the efficiency of Union decision making (Von Weizsäcker, Dehaene and Simon 1999).

Consequently the Nice Treaty made several adaptations to the provisions on CC. A joint paper by the German and Italian governments known as the Schröder-Amato paper set out certain key changes to CC as part of the pre-Nice deliberations, and these changes were eventually agreed by the entire set of member states. Indeed, the Biarritz summit of 13–14 October 2000, which was held to prepare the way for agreements at the later Nice summit, reached an agreement that the ToN would include revisions to the CC mechanism—a remarkable achievement given the fact that the Nice summit itself almost failed to produce a new Treaty in the face of unprecedented degrees of in-fighting and dissatisfaction within the European Council on other issues (notably the member states' respective voting weights). Continuing the trend towards seeing flexibility as a tool of policy/polity management rather than an ideological principle, the member states appear to have reached agreement on reform rather easily—although by the same token CC was not given a radical overhaul.

As noted by Gillespie (2001), the latest Treaty in fact raises several barriers to the effective implementation of CC. These are as follows: it cannot introduce new competences to the EU's preserve; it cannot apply to matters in which the EU has exclusive competence; it must not distort the single market or adversely affect socio-economic cohesion; it must not be used as a first choice policy instrument, but rather may serve as one of last resort; it must remain open to those member states which initially opt-out but subsequently wish to take part; it must serve to reinforce the general integration process. In addition, CC must continue to ensure that the competences, rights and duties of non-participant member states are respected (European Parliament 2001). These factors obviously act as a restraint on member states eager to form a closely-knit vanguard group, preserving some of the bargain struck at Amsterdam. Furthermore, the Nice Treaty explicitly sets a limit on the use of flexibility in pillar 2; although the possible range of the latter was extended, it is explicitly ruled out in matters with defence or military implications, meaning that progress in this area will continue to be coloured significantly by an extra-EU dimension. Above all, reforms to closer cooperation were accompanied by a new emphasis on solidarity, or at least the idea of 'economic and social cohesion' which is the EU's Treaty equivalent (Gillespie 2001). Thus, while CC was facilitated, this was done within a framework of procedural and normative restrictions which must be borne in mind.

However, this should not be taken to imply that the adaptations made in the ToN were insignificant. As far as the issue of the triggering mechanism is concerned, the abolition of the national veto power in pillars 1 and 3 was a crucial innovation, since it thereby removes the ability of a single recalcitrant state to block progress, echoing the reinstatement of QMV which was such a significant part of the Single European Act. Moreover, the EP was granted a role in approving the launch of CC in pillar 1, by the assent procedure (if the EP would enjoy codecision rights over the subsequent legislation). This removed many of the concerns about the implications of CC for the democratic deficit. In pillar 2, the High Representative of the Council is tasked with a duty to inform both the EP and all the member states (including non-participants) about the progress of CC measures. In pillar 3, the Council will now both approve the launch of a CC measure and decide whether initially laggard states can subsequently join it by QMV, on the basis of a proposal from the Commission, thus facilitating decision making and increasing the likelihood of CC measures being undertaken. The Nice Treaty also gives the Commission a partial veto power under pillar 3,[3] similar to that which it already enjoyed under Amsterdam in the case of the first pillar.

Clauses A–F of the Nice Treaty set out general principles which are applicable to any CC measure regardless of the pillar in which it is undertaken. Thus, there is some degree of procedural standardization. The quorum for a CC initiative is set at eight, rather than a majority of the member states; although the two currently coincide (since at the time of the ToN there were fifteen member states), it is the exact number rather than the requirement for a majority which is now in the Treaty. Thus, after the next enlargement, CC need involve less than half the number of member states, a decision which further increases the prospects that CC might actually be used. The Treaty no longer requires CC not to cause discrimination between EU citizens or have an adverse impact on EU citizenship, a step which appears entirely sensible since such a requirement was worthless in real terms except as a barrier to closer cooperation—flexibility cannot help creating differences, and thus potential inequalities, between the nationals of participant and non-participant member states. However, the new requirement to respect socio-economic cohesion may mean that CC continues to suffer similarly under the Nice Treaty.

The definition of 'last resort' was slightly clarified by the Nice Treaty (European Parliament 2001), thereby indicating that a degree of political judgment and interpretation can be exercised over the issue: the Council is empowered by Clause B to decide when the objectives of a proposed vanguard group cannot be met by the traditional

---

3.   Under the Nice Treaty, if the Commission refuses officially to propose a CC measure in pillar 3, it must state its reasons, and this rationale is subject to appeal in the European Council by the member state which had sought the measure.

Community method 'within a reasonable period'. This addition of a time limit is crucial—it implies that the Council will be allowed to endorse CC, by qualified majority, not only on the grounds that the traditional approach is unsuitable but also on the basis that even when the latter could be used it could not meet the required goals with sufficient speed. Thus, *perceived efficiency becomes the key factor in making decisions to allow CC*, and opponents of flexibility have had their case made more difficult to argue, at least as far as secondary legislation is concerned.

The Nice Treaty ensures that CC operations remain open to those member states which initially opt out, and adds that both participating member states and the Commission are called upon to encourage them to take part (European Parliament 2001). It generally preserves the decision rules set out in the Amsterdam Treaty (only participating member states may vote in Council, with the other institutions empowered as if the CC measure were one in which all member states participate), although it stipulates that CC measures and decisions are not to be considered part of the Union *acquis*. Similarly, it preserves the financing arrangements originally agreed (costs are to be borne by participating member states, unless there is unanimous agreement in the Council to bear the costs from the EU budget). Thus, the Nice Treaty ensures that 'the EU is now equipped with a reasonably operational mechanism for closer cooperation' (Philippart 2001: 7).

Remaining Problems of Closer Cooperation

Nonetheless, there remain shortcomings in the way closer cooperation has been operationalized. This is not in itself surprising; like everything else in European integration, at least to date, closer cooperation is work in progress and thus liable to periodic re-evaluation. As Philippart (2001) argues, the Nice Treaty was able to make progress on CC because it was seen to be a relatively non-controversial issue. At Amsterdam, only a few of the member states had sought to codify flexibility, and were thus forced to make many concessions to those states which were either opposed to this or cautious. By the time of Nice, with enlargement that much closer (the Treaty negotiations actually dealt with the issue of the respective voting weights in Council and numbers of seats in the EP of the candidate countries), CC was more readily presentable as an essential tool of diversity management.

Moreover, the prospect of further enlargement soothed the concerns of many member states which had feared ending up in a second division of membership, given the fact that the likely new entrants all face greater difficulties in applying the *acquis* than any of the current member states. In addition, those member states opposed to closer co-operation at Amsterdam had there extracted so many concessions that they considered it safe at Nice to allow something of a relaxation of the controls on CC as part of the general bargaining process, even when their opposition to flexibility remained strong (Philippart 2001).

Thus, the approach taken at Nice was to endorse moderate facilita-tion of closer cooperation. Several key issues remain to be addressed.[4] First, it may be that the triggering mechanism is still too clumsy. Although the national veto has been abolished, granting the EP power to approve the launch of CC if it enjoys codecision powers in the relevant subsequent legislation adds a further complication and a further hurdle to be cleared. Although there is no question that CC must not remove the EP's legislative powers, it is not so clear that the Parliament should be so empowered over its launch, especially when the role of the Commission remains so great. It is true that codecision has managed to empower the EP without causing too great a delay in decision making, but in the case of legislation the EP has everything to gain from clever use of its powers. In terms of approving CC measures which might otherwise have to be enacted under more traditional methods, it is not clear whether the EP would perceive gains to lie in allowing the launch. Parliament's default position might thus be to refuse assent. Two factors are crucial here. First, it is possible that the growing common legislative culture between Council and EP which has been caused by codecision (Shackleton 2000) might prove possible to extend to common interinstitutional thinking about CC. Second, and more onerously, the relevant member states may seek to blackmail the EP by a threat to cooperate outside the Union framework if no approval to use CC is granted—in which case, the EP would lose out signi-ficantly. Thus, this issue requires careful exploration.

A separate issue is the flexibility of CC itself, that is, its existence in multiple forms. Although it is by no means the case that flexibility must operate in entirely the same fashion in each pillar, the arrangements for pillar 2 are needlessly complex. Matters of the common foreign and

4. See Chapter 4 for further exploration of the problems of flexibility in general.

security policy are always likely to be sensitive, and there is no need to suppose that, for example, the Commission should have its full range of powers in this pillar until and unless the member states move closer to a common policy than they are brought even by the Rapid Reaction Force—the institutional impact of which is likely to be massive in terms of the culture and ethos of the Council, and also in relations between Council and Commission. There is no evident reason why arrangements similar to those which apply in pillar 3 could not also extend to the second pillar, however.

Additionally, the requirement that CC measures respect social and economic cohesion must be clarified, at least informally, since currently this could be construed as a barrier to launching CC should a sufficient number of the member states, the Commission or the EP so choose. Such ambiguity does, of course, allow for situation-specific judgments, which thus implies that some progress will be possible—and official clarification of what constitutes damage to cohesion might be so restrictive as to impede any significant use of CC. Nonetheless, at least informally, actors in the Commission, EP and Council must come to some agreement about this since their approbation is necessary for CC to be operated in the first pillar.

Another crucial issue is the fact that even after Nice closer cooperation cannot be used to add new competences to the Union's remit. Thus, much of the potential of flexibility is not likely to be tapped via its incarnation as CC: despite the fact that EMU shows that flexibility can be used to deepen integration and carry with it the great majority of the member states, such a use of flexibility still requires the sanction of an intergovernmental conference and Treaty reform. Much can of course be achieved via cooperation under existing policy competences —social policy is a potential case in point—but it is clear that CC will not be able to allow groups of member states to take the Union in radical new directions.

For that very reason, closer cooperation is unlikely to be able to prevent member states cooperating outside the Union institutions. Member states have always done this, and they may always do so. Given the limits of Union competence, and certain worthwhile ties between member states which pre-date their accession to the Union (for instance the currency union between Belgium and Luxembourg— although this is of course now superseded by EMU), such cooperation is often necessary. However, advocates of flexibility have tended to justify it on the grounds that it can allow deepening (Tindemans 1976; Dewatripont *et al.* 1995); should this not prove correct it is by no means necessarily the case that member states seeking progress would use their frustration to push for further reform of CC. Instead, they might resort to more extensive extra-EU cooperation, a step which would deprive the EU institutions of their powers over resultant legislation.

Finally, CC cannot be applied to existing parts of the *acquis*. Thus, member states cannot unravel their existing commitments and responsibilities in the name of flexibility, at least not without Treaty reform approved by intergovernmental summit. While this is a sensible precaution when applied to existing member states, it is less clear that the same rigidity should apply to candidate countries, many of whose accession could be sped up by decisions to opt-out of certain parts of the *acquis* (de la Serre and Wallace 1997), an option already granted, *de facto* if not *de jure*, to Sweden over the single currency.

Thus, closer cooperation remains incompletely elaborated and likely to face further reform. Its trajectory from Amsterdam to Nice has seen the first constitutionalization of flexibility, and its subsequent reform and partial facilitation. In the next chapter I explore the remaining problems further.

4 |

Problems of Flexibility

Introduction

In this chapter I discuss the problems commonly associated with the use of flexibility as a central feature of European integration. This is because these problems become most salient, and thus most in need of resolution, if flexibility is invoked systematically rather than as an ad hoc practice. The remaining issues are manifold; as detailed in Chapter 3, 'closer cooperation' remains imperfectly articulated. Furthermore, flexibility continues to inspire hostility, or at least great concern, in many observers and practitioners of European integration. Many of those committed to European integration as a process of state-building continue to view flexibility as the antithesis of their objectives, and one which is thus to be avoided at all costs. Thus, in some quarters, opposition to flexibility is a default response, although in order to keep up with events this is transforming into an attempt to ensure that flexibility is limited to multi-speed models (Duff 1997a; Von Weizsäcker, Dehaene and Simon 1999). Moreover, it cannot be denied that flexibility poses problems of polity management which range from the predominantly administrative (ensuring the more variegated polity is 'policed' effectively) to the legal (further challenges to the supremacy of EC law) and the normative (issues of democracy, as problems of reduced transparency and solidarity are evident).

However, I argue that in fact the greatest danger of flexibility is that it will become yet another potentially useful principle of Union governance which fails to become sufficiently operationalized, much like subsidiarity. Much of the integration process in Europe is shaped by a practice of 'muddling through'—the avoidance of key decisions as often as possible, and response to immediate need rather than elaboration of a detailed strategy for action over the medium to long term. Thus, key principles are often deliberately left ambiguous, in order to accommodate different member state views, and also to allow for further development at a subsequent, and more propitious, time. That this approach also applies to flexibility is evident in the changes made to closer cooperation at the Nice Summit, an event which also clearly signalled that the gradualist approach can, and does, produce progress. There is much to be said for an ongoing evolution of Union governance both strategically and normatively: it allows actors to revisit and recast earlier bargains, and also permits by iteration the establishment of a more deeply entrenched culture of negotiation and dialogue, itself necessary to produce common understandings and underpin reform. However, gradualism must not be an excuse for neglect of, or refusal to tackle, difficult problems. The normative and operational bases of flexibility must be further clarified; even after the changes wrought at Nice, closer cooperation reflects the logics of all three main models of flexibility (see Chapter 1), and the problem of its underdetermined normative underpinnings identified by Jo Shaw (1998) remains in evidence. Thus, in this chapter I argue that the opportunity to address key issues of European integration provided by the 'post-Nice' process must be used to make further progress on the operationalization of flexibility, even if such progress would (or should) omit to make absolutely definitive decisions on that, or indeed any, score.

The structure of the chapter is as follows. In the next section I discuss what might be termed 'general' problems of flexibility such as the need to choose between—or perhaps balance more successfully—the different models. Subsequently I look at 'policy style' issues, asking whether flexibility has implications for the growing trend towards 'soft policy' and for the EU's own suitability as a useful policy instrument in the context of pan-European governance. Finally, I look in turn at three of the greatest challenges posed by flexibility in vital areas of Union governance: external policy, EC law, and democracy.

General Problems of Flexibility: Member State Relations

Perhaps the greatest, and most obvious, problem of flexibility is that it adds to the already impressive complexity of the EU's structures. The EU has always been characterized by the novelty of its institutional arrangements and by the extent to which its policy-making process is interinstitutional, even if the member governments have always collectively retained the key role (for an overview, see Warleigh 2001a).

There are several decision-making processes within the EU's 'single institutional framework', with the European Parliament being empowered to differing degrees. The dynamics of the relationship between the political and legal institutions are often Byzantine, with the Court of Justice often able to exert significant influence over the course of integration, but with the member states also often ready to 'rein in' the Court's influence (see Hunt 2001 for an overview). The degree to which the Union is subject to change, and its reliance upon informal politics to make good the 'gaps' in its institutional structure, are both high. Thus, the introduction of flexibility is likely to compound an already complex situation, and pose significant challenges of manageability—even if the rules for the operationalization of closer cooperation are made rather simpler than they are currently.[1]

As a consequence it is necessary to address further issues of an institutional nature—especially the question of who should be responsible for the management of closer cooperation activities and the need to ensure that they are well governed. Here, the problem is that member governments which seek to work as a sub-group of the Union may decide that they wish to exert complete control over such cooperation, and thereby deliberately exclude the Commission, Parliament and Court. There is even something of a precedent for this in the evolving form of the pillar structure; pillars 2 and 3 involve the EP and Court scarcely at all, and give only a small role to the Commission. There is no *a priori* need for this to be the case, however, and indeed the underlying logic of the EU—that is, its fundamental nature as a progressive confederation reliant upon the delegation of semi-independent powers to EU institutions by the contracting states (Forsyth 1981; Warleigh 2000a)—implies that the member states would in all likelihood seek to ensure that the Commission and Court are empowered to ensure the smooth functioning of the system. There is equally a precedent for this in the arrangements for closer cooperation made at Nice, which task the Commission with ensuring that measures enacted using the CC provisions are fundamentally in line with, or at least not

1. See Kortenberg (1998) and Stubb (1997) for different, and more positive, views of the arrangements for closer cooperation under the Amsterdam Treaty. According to both these authors, it is commonplace to exaggerate both the difficulties and the dangers of closer cooperation, a view which is certainly likely to become more general after the Nice reforms.

in contradiction to, the relevant *acquis*. Similarly, the emergent consensus that neither the Commission nor the EP should be considered
'non-collegiate' for the purposes of closer cooperation—that is, that
MEPs and Commissioners from member states which opt out should be
allowed to participate as normal in their respective institution's role in
decision making (Neunreither 2000)—implies that this management
function will not necessarily be carried out intergovernmentally. Nonetheless, there remain important issues of institutional resources to bear
in mind. Should closer cooperation become the means by which the
Union produces a significantly greater volume of legislation, both the
Commission and the Parliament—not to mention the Court—will
require further resources in order to carry out their tasks effectively.
Moreover, there will certainly be a need for all the institutions to adapt
to further new ways of working which revisit the balancing act between
intergovernmental choice (here, to enact and join a CC measure) with
supranational responsibility for policy/polity management.

Another general problem is that of the relationship between those
member states which decide to press ahead with a measure under closer
cooperation, and those which remain outside. Wessels (1998) raises an
issue apparent in the history of the relationship between the UK and the
EU, namely the fact that not having participated at the start of the
process has made the UK resentful of rules and legislation by which it
is bound but which it did not co-shape; instead, the UK was consigned
to a long process of playing catch-up, and, at least partly as a result, has
been less *communautaire* in its outlook than most of the other member
states.[2] Whether or not the British case is fully capable of translation to
other, perhaps more traditionally pro-integration member states is an
issue for debate. However, there are justifiable concerns that a country
which initially opts out may find it hard to join the vanguard group later
on—if only because it will have to rubber-stamp a raft of measures
which it might have wished were cast very differently. This, of course,
returns us to the need for sound management of closer cooperation
discussed immediately above.

A related issue is that of the criteria to be applied in either launching
closer cooperation, or deciding to opt out. The European Court of

---

2.   There are of course other, additional reasons for the traditionally cautious
British approach to European integration—see, *inter alia*, Young 1998; George
1994.

Justice has to date failed to accept that political will, rather than failure to meet a specified set of entry criteria, is acceptable as a means of opting out of secondary legislation (Tuytschaever 2000). But in decisions of primary legislation (Treaty reform) it has no voice, a fact which enables member states to opt out on that very basis—for example, the UK's non-participation in the single currency despite successful meeting of the criteria spelled out in the Maastricht Treaty. There is genuine need for further clarity about which kinds of policy require participants to be able to meet certain stipulated entrance tests, and those which do not. There also remains a need to clarify who should be responsible for making decisions about which of the non-participants is able to join the vanguard, a responsibility currently split between the Commission and the Council. Where clear functional criteria are set out, these decisions are best given to a supranational body, where the chances of neutral judgment are perhaps higher; however, where the issue is purely whether the vanguard is happy to extend membership of the club—and thus a political matter—the decision should rest with the Council. This would have the merit of making responsibility for the decision clear. In cases where an application is rejected, the Council should be obliged to produce a written and detailed reason, which should be subject to appeal at the Court of Justice.

A further, and closely linked, issue of relations between the member states posed by flexibility is that of which model of flexibility is applied. Concentric circles models set out a vision of a Union divided into several clear tiers of membership rather like a football league; member states would have to choose which tier of membership they want, rather than make decisions based on specific policies (as would be the case for multi-speed and à la carte models). This is an important distinction because a member state in a tier of membership which is significantly less integrated than the arrangements for the 'hard core' states is likely to find it difficult to address the very problems raised by Wessels: the hard core would start well ahead, and probably move even further away over time. If such a situation results from the deliberate and free choice of the 'peripheral' state, however, then the significance of the problem is much reduced. If a state finds itself unwillingly on the periphery of the Union, the issue is much more problematic. This is a fear held by many 'small' member states (Gillespie 1997)—but, shifting focus momentarily to praxis—the participation of most of these states in the single currency should in fact mean that they are only on the margins through choice.[3]

Traditionally, the means of preventing such problems has been to advocate multi-speed rather than multi-tier forms of flexibility, in which the vanguard states have a responsibility to help the others to join the lead group (Tindemans 1976). However, the current signs are that such solidarity is not present. For example, the Spanish refusal at Nice to allow renegotiation of the fundamentals of the EU budget until 2007 may well mean that a thorough revision of the budgetary aspects of the common agricultural and regional policies is impossible to implement before 2013: if so, Spain has thereby ensured that it will retain what will be a disproportionate share of Union financial contributions despite the Nice commitment to undertake the first wave of enlargement to the Central and East European candidate countries, which should objectively benefit most from those policies, by 2004. Moreover, multi-speed models do not address the fundamental rationale of flexibility, that is, the issue of deliberate member state choice not to participate (Junge 1999). Thus, the issue of which model of flexibility is appropriate for the EU must be addressed in order to make explicit (and thus subject to public debate) the relations that the member states envisage between themselves.

The Question of 'Policy Style'

Flexibility also poses interesting questions about the nature of the EU as a tool for meeting policy objectives. These can be summed up along three axes: the EU's relationship with other 'European' governance regimes; the mixture of 'soft' and 'hard' policy; and the issue of whether or not certain policy areas must be placed outside the scope of closer cooperation or indeed any other kind of flexibility. Thus, flexibility raises issues of the appropriate 'policy style' for the EU.

The first of these conundrums essentially revolves around the question of how the EU fits alongside the other inter- or transnational regimes in Europe as a means by which the member states choose to pursue their policy objectives, as in Schmitter's 1996 model of the 'condominio'. Indeed, flexibility brings this issue more squarely onto

---

3.   Denmark remains of course the exception, although so far its non-participation in the vanguard of the Union has been through explicit choice at both elite and popular levels.

the agenda than before, since it realizes that member states are likely to continue their participation in such regimes rather than seek to subsume all of them in a new EU federation. The implication of flexibility is that the coexistence of the Union with such regimes is likely to be ongoing in the medium to long term, and that—as with the Franco-British St Malo initiative in defence policy—this coexistence can actually be beneficial to the Union.

However, this coexistence also presents a challenge, in that the Union faces competition from other potential cooperative regimes—but many supporters of flexibility argue that the primary benefit of closer cooperation has been its apparent de-legitimization of extra-EU cooperation by the member states. Wessels (1998) usefully and sympathetically sums up such thinking by writing that closer cooperation might build up pressure for a return to the traditional Community Method (or, perhaps, at least its more democratic variant which features a stronger role for the EP), since CC is difficult to manage and also makes clearer who the 'free riders' in any situation are. In turn, this reduces the attractiveness of such an option for states who wish not to participate. In time, the member states might come to regret their experiment and go back to their more habitual forms of joint legislation and problem-solving. Thus, there is a mismatch between the inherent dynamics of flexibility and the use to which actors within the institutions of the Union may seek to put it. However, as the Treaty specifically outlaws the use of closer cooperation to add new competences to the *acquis*, it is difficult to see how the provisions on closer cooperation can be used to prevent extra-EU collaboration by member states either legally or normatively (Tuytschaever 1999; Kortenberg 1998). Thus, the Union will continue to constitute one part of a complex latticework of institutions, and its own evolution will in part be shaped by that of its institutional context.

Such an argument as Wessels' is allied to the perspective of those who are concerned by the Union's increasing tendency to complement the traditional ways of working in the Union with other approaches to policy making—the five modes of governance defined by Wallace (2000b) as the Community method, the regulatory approach, multilevel governance, policy coordination/benchmarking and 'intensive transgovernmentalism'. These modes of governance reflect the general tendency in recent political life to reduce, or at least alter, the role of the state or its equivalent. Ironically, flexibility and these changing policy modes combine to pose a threat to both advocates of the traditional approach to integration (the state-in-waiting perspective, in which deeper European integration is always a normative good in its own right) and more recent converts, who view European integration as a means by which global neoliberalism could be diluted by the creation of a stronger EU social policy (Therborn 1997). The 'soft' policy modes identified by Wallace are certainly open to challenge on normative grounds—for example, Scharpf (1999) argues convincingly that their use has led to an erosion of welfare policies at the member state level which has not been made good at the EU level. However, it is necessary to separate social democratic concerns from those of institutional actors in the integration process; the two neither coincide nor diverge automatically. It is true that the social dimension of European integration is underdeveloped; however, it is by no means clear that many advocates of deeper integration have sought its entrenchment as more than an instrumental device by which the overall scope of integration would be augmented, with the latter being the primary objective. In fact, it must remain a possibility that flexibility could actually do more to allow the development of social competence at EU level by allowing the more neoliberal states to opt out of, rather than oppose, such measures—as was the case for the Social Charter.

In turn, this brings us to a further puzzle: is flexibility objectively suitable for some policies, and not others? As mentioned above, it is now fairly common for commentators to acknowledge the utility of flexibility if it is placed within certain clear confines (Dewatripont *et al.* 1995; Ehlermann 1995; Curtin 1997; Junge 1999). According to this logic, flexibility is for use as an instrument rather than as an end in itself (Ehlermann 1995), and is acceptable only as a means of last resort used to unblock the integration process, thereby allowing those member states who wish to, to integrate further. It must not erode the achievements of the integration process to date by unravelling key bargains and compromises—an approach reflected by the Treaty injunction that closer cooperation cannot be used to unpick the *acquis*. Moreover, flexibility should be accompanied by an agreement about core policy areas which must be tackled by the whole EU. Most observers consider that such a 'core Europe' should consist of the single market and the truly necessary flanking measures. However, given the fact that both political and legal institutions of the Union have used the single market as justification for the creation of new EU competences and even legal rights (see, for example, the judgment of the Court of Justice in *Cowan v. Le Trésor Public*, case 186/87 [1989] ECR 195), and also the continuing differences between the member governments on precisely this issue, it is difficult to see what could constitute an objective limit to the 'truly necessary' flanking measures.[4] Indeed, de Búrca (2000) shows that even the single market has been subject to some degree of flexibility, which means that this supposedly sacrosanct part of the Union's work has been viewed with less deference than might be imagined. Interestingly, however, there is no clear signal, since the Treaty provisions which currently approximate to serving this purpose (definition of scope) are very restrictive. For instance, Junge (1999) argues that the Amsterdam Treaty effectively defined the common base as all the current *acquis*, plus those areas in which the EU has exclusive competence, a far larger set of policies than is likely to emerge from any explicit negotiation on the matter.

Thus, flexibility involves several difficult problems for the Union on the issue of policy style: its relationship with other inter- and trans-national regimes; the kind of approach to policy making it should adopt; and the definition of the policy areas in which flexibility is considered acceptable, an issue which is explored further below.

External Policy and Flexibility

One of the main worries about flexibility is its potential to undermine the Union's ability to capitalize on its growing powers by translating them into an effective voice on the world stage. This is because the issues of international political economy in which the EU rather than the individual member states is active require it to speak with a single voice if it is to be effective. For example, Smith (2000) argues that the internal complexity of the Union means that it is already suboptimally effective as an international negotiator, since it must assemble internal coalitions for each issue, and may not be able to sustain that coalition either over time or across different issues at any given moment. By extension, increasing the internal diversity of the Union may lead to greater problems of the same type, and return the 'Who speaks for Europe?' question to the top of the agenda just when other develop-ments in pillar 2 are pushing towards a solution to that problem in

4. See Dewatripont *et al.* (1995) for perhaps the most detailed of these schemes.

foreign policy matters through the appointment of a High Representative (currently Javier Solana).

Charles Grant (2000) argues along similar lines, maintaining that
while flexibility is permissible (and perhaps even necessary) in *defence*
policy given the fact that several of the Union's member states are
neutral, it is completely out of the question in EU *foreign* policy, since
the latter is simply not credible if certain member states adopt a different position. Dashwood (1996: 166) supports this point of view,
arguing that an EU claiming to represent all member states but in fact
only representing a sub-group of them would have little influence, since
third countries could simply exploit the differences between the
positions of the member states.

Dashwood also notes that since the EU can assume competence in
areas of external policy if this is necessary to achieve the objectives of
an internal policy, it is possible that conflicts of interest might arise
between different groupings of member states. Those involved in a case
of 'domestic' flexibility may not support the relevant external policy of
the EU; alternatively, a policy which involves all the member states
internally may involve only a sub-group of them externally, leading to
resource and policy content difficulties. Similarly, it could be argued
that the distinction drawn by Grant between foreign and defence
policies is exaggerated; by no means all foreign policy has defence
connotations, but given the New Security Agenda (which has both
allowed progress in EU foreign policy and also re-emphasized the EU's
role in 'soft', or economic, diplomacy), the links between the internal
market and its defence by various mechanisms at the global level must
be borne in mind. The EU often uses economic tools to achieve foreign
policy goals—particularly, but not exclusively, via the World Trade
Organization (WTO) and in development policy.

Thus there are certainly problems associated with flexibility on the
issue of the EU's role in the world. Flexibility is primarily a tool for the
advancement of internal integration, a means by which the member
states agree to disagree about their differences but permit at least
certain of their number to press ahead with an objective which they
share as a sub-group. Clearly, it makes the Union likely to become a
more differentiated system, even if that system is partially and even
generally deepened. However, two corollaries must be borne in mind.
First, the main tool of making foreign policy at the Union level (outside
the 'purely' economic realm) has so far been the attempt to make sure

the member states consult each other about their various objectives, and thus produce policies which do not flatly contradict each other (as was the case for European Political Cooperation): it has met with very limited success.[5] Thus, flexibility may allow further progress by involving only those member states which truly support a strong role for the Union in this policy area and which have developed sufficient common interests to make such a démarche viable. Second, the EU continues to operate its defence policy within the orbit of NATO—even the Rapid Reaction Force (RRF) is only to be deployed using NATO resources, and when NATO itself chooses not to act. Three considerations suggest themselves as a result. First, the issue of the EU's coherence as an independent defence policy actor is less important within the NATO context (although clearly it is vital that any action by the RRF is effective). Second, different modes of flexibility are actually the key reason why the EU has made progress in foreign policy in recent years—extra-EU cooperation by France and the UK made what became the RRF a possibility (Hoffmann 2000), and within NATO that same RRF will act as a 'European' sub-group. Thus, flexibility and external policy are not necessarily incompatible. Third, the impossibility of drawing a clear distinction between internal and external policies certainly poses difficulties for the EU, but as Dashwood himself points out (1996: 166), this actually represents a need to construct innovative legal structures rather than an insurmountable barrier to either the elaboration of flexibility or the deepening of cooperation in external policy.

Flexibility and EC Law

However, flexibility does present serious challenges to traditional views of EC law. Many legal scholars have tended to view EC law as detached from, and somehow purer than, EU politics—a force for integration which is objective and focused on the needs of the system rather than the interests of any member state. Incontrovertibly, law has been an instrument which binds the member states together in the Union; at a very basic level, EC law is what allows the member states

5.   In more 'economic' matters, the EU has pursued an increasingly differentiated policy with success, pursuing a coherent overall agenda despite initiating different kinds of relations with different (groups of) third countries (Cremona 2000).

to establish common ways of working and ensure that the system they jointly create is both capable of oversight and able to ensure that they all play, more or less, by the same rules.

Although traditional views in EC legal studies are often guilty of 'overstating…the degree of perfection and the coherence of purpose achieved by the Court of Justice in its interpretations of EC law' and of 'conflating the role of that Court with the legal order itself' (Armstrong and Shaw 1998: 148), they do contain some validity. The judgments of the ECJ have often been significant in shaping the direction of the integration process, both in relation to particular policy areas and as a source of greatly important principles such as direct effect and supremacy[6] which have created a solid legal order for the Union (Hunt 2001). Indeed, at certain stages in the integration process, it has arguably been the judgments of the Court which have set the pace, or at least sustained the Union in otherwise fairly fallow periods—sometimes provoking opposing action by the Council (Taylor 1975). Although it is unclear whether the Court consciously considers itself to be activist in the integration process or whether it is simply the case that ECJ judgments have had a system-shaping effect in the absence of a deliberate strategy to shape the wider integration process (Hunt 2001), it is clear that without the Court's contribution the integration process would be less advanced.

This has led many legal scholars to be suspicious of flexibility, since it is likely to unravel the carefully constructed, relatively uniform legal order. By envisaging the establishment of coexisting subsystems with multiple relationships to the main body of the *acquis*, flexibility undermines the idea that EC law should be a means of harmonization. Indeed, flexibility can be read as antithetical to the role of the Court. For instance, Ehlermann (1984) argues that EC law itself has long been differentiated to the extent that directives (and even regulations) permit the member states to find their own means of implementation. Consequently, provided that legal differentiation is time-bound (and thus applied to particular pieces of legislation rather than erected as a general principle), this poses no problem to the EC legal order. However, for Ehlermann even the multi-speed model of integration challenges this order because it results from political choice; given the differen-

---

6.   Direct effect is the doctrine that EC law provides rights and duties directly into national law, which national courts must protect; supremacy is the doctrine that if EC law and national law are in conflict, EC law prevails.

tiation permissible under EC law, any attempt to take the principle of flexibility further indicates a deliberate decision to enshrine diversity instead of harmonization, political choice rather than legal obligation.

Ehlermann later modified this view, arguing that multi-speed approaches are compatible with EC law, but concentric circles and à la carte models are not, since multi-speed models explicitly envisage eventual uniformity and see flexibility as a means to an end rather than an end in itself (Ehlermann 1995). In this revised view, should multi-speed models be employed, it would be vital to ensure that the EU institutions are used as regularly as possible, and that extra-EU cooperation is thereby minimized. Moreover, a clear set of core areas in which flexibility would not be permitted must be established. However, it must be admitted that in any case flexibility could well undermine two key principles which the ECJ holds dear: non-discrimination between member states, and supremacy of EC law (Tuytschaever 1999). Closer cooperation writes an exception to the former into primary law, that is, the Treaty; it also implies that national government choice to opt out is of greater importance than uniform obligations under EC law. The ad hoc development of flexibility so far has clearly caused legal problems, such as how suitable boundaries and bridging mechanisms should be set up between the various parts of the legal order (Walker 2000).

In fact, EC law has a double function regarding flexibility. In one sense, it is subordinated to political choice, to the extent that member states make ad hoc arrangements rather than systematic choices for the use of flexibility; in another, it plays a role in ensuring system efficiency, since member states have established the rules for closer cooperation as a means of making flexibility work in practice, as well as more intelligible (Walker 2000). Indeed, by setting up the rules for CC, the member states allowed the Court of Justice a role in policing its operation in the first pillar, a power which the Court does not have regarding flexibility in matters of Treaty change such as the Maastricht opt-outs (de Búrca 2000). Thus, in an EU system whose legal complexity is set to increase, the Court may become an ever more vital actor, with a role in shaping new conceptions of legal order (Lyons 2000): in order to ensure that those member states which initially press ahead with a policy initiative respect the rights of those which are obliged to wait—and vice versa—the ECJ should be empowered to act as an arbiter in cases of alleged malpractice (Ehlermann 1995; Curtin 1997).

Consequently, while flexibility poses problems for both the EC legal order and the ECJ itself, it does not necessarily imply the sidelining of either, at least in pillar 1. Instead, it marks the European process as one which is 'essentially contested', in which persistent conflict over norms is to be expected rather than deliberately eradicated—a view which is possible to reconcile with a strong legal order, but one which is conceived rather differently, and less hierarchically, than in the past (Bañkowski and Scott 1998; MacCormick 1999).

Flexibility and Democracy

It is perhaps on the question of democracy that flexibility is most often subject to criticism. Flexibility is all about allowing difference, and possibly (as a consequence) inequalities. As noted above, this challenges the legal principle of non-discrimination between member states. Flexibility also takes the EU away from traditional views of a federal end product of integration with a uniform constitutional settlement, at least in the medium term. It can be seen to make the EU more complicated as a system, and thus less transparent. In this view, a flexible, that is, even more differentiated, system may be less easy to make accountable (since transparency problems will make it less clear who is responsible for what); it may also decrease levels of popular participation, since citizens who cannot understand the system are less likely to engage with it (Ehlermann 1998). These are most definitely crucial issues for the EU, whose democratic legitimacy has been subject to increasing and sustained criticism since the signing of the Maastricht Treaty.

Part of the problem is that flexibility has come to the fore at precisely this historical juncture. For a Union with damaged credibility and where increased intergovernmentalism (or at least changes in policy modes) appears evident, it is easy for those who support further progress towards 'ever closer union' to see flexibility as part of a general attempt to reduce the scope and level of integration in the name of national sovereignty. Certainly, although the most recent Commission Presidents (Santer and Prodi) have committed themselves to a 'less, but better' approach to integration, it is clear that flexibility can be represented in a Eurosceptic light as the defence of national autonomy against the rapacious onslaught of 'Brussels'—such thinking is obvious in the position of the UK Conservative party, for example. Academic work has also been informed by this logic; in their detailed proposals for operationalizing flexibility, Dewatripont *et al.* (1995) consider that democracy in the EU is primarily a matter of equality of opportunity and voice between member states rather than citizens, whose interests are pursued by national governments.

In terms of democratic theory, such views contain a distinct element of communitarianism—the perspective that democracy is only possible within the confines of a closely-knit community defined by common history/destiny, values and culture, with these often (but by no means always) in turn seen to depend on blood ties of either kinship, ethnicity and/or nationality (Walzer 1994; Miller 1995). A deep sense of community is seen to be necessary because unless individuals identify with each other they are unlikely to develop attributes of reciprocity and mutual trust, the conditions for minority acceptance of majority rule. If there are serious conflicts between citizens, community is what, at base, permits their peaceful and mutually acceptable resolution. The ultimate form of political community is seen by communitarians to be the nation state, which combines community (nation) with effective means of governance (the state); thus, international organizations must not undermine either nation or state, or they thereby imperil democracy. Consequently the EU must be kept within certain confines; flexibility, read as opting out, is the natural and necessary use of national sovereignty to protect democracy from being subsumed in an over-arching technocracy which could never develop the necessary sense of community. Thus, flexibility-as-national-sovereignty is seen by communitarians as entirely democratic; for many integrationists,[7] however, it appears totally the opposite: the privileging of national (elite?) interests over those of the EU as a whole, and a deliberate ploy to prevent the progressive development of a European, rather than national, sense of community and mutual belonging.

However, as with EC law, it is possible to consider flexibility as emblematic of a different, and potentially preferable, view of how democratization within the EU can best be effectuated. The EU is a

---

7.   The school of thought which opposes communitarianism is cosmopolitanism —the belief that democracy beyond borders is not only possible but necessary, and based on human rights rather than territorial belonging. Cosmopolitans tend to support the idea of world (rather than regional) government; it is thus questionable whether all proponents of European integration are really cosmopolitan, or simply wishing to build a regional state. For an overview of how cosmopolitanism and communitarianism apply to the EU context, see Bellamy and Warleigh 1998.

system of multi-level governance, whose legitimacy must draw on both governmental and popular sources as well as the supranational level (Höreth 1999). Thus, while communitarianism is insufficient as a philosophy of EU democracy, it points out certain variables which are likely to be necessary in the democratization process, such as the need for a relatively 'thick' sense of community (albeit politically rather than ethnically defined) and the need to take the normative claims of national autonomy seriously, even if they can be articulated in a very exaggerated way. In this perspective, the fact that flexibility permits and enshrines difference is seen to have great normative value (Warleigh 2002). In other words, because flexibility does not seek a uniform outcome but instead allows member states to experiment with different forms of governance, it allows governments to concentrate on what unites them rather than what separates them. Flexibility also accepts that certain differences between the views of the member states (and their publics) about the desirable end product of integration, and their respective contribution to it, may be permanent; given the existence of such difference, certain democratic theorists consider that seeking to impose uniformity is normatively unacceptable, and that instead it is necessary to reach mutually acceptable outcomes by a process of iterated dialogue and gradualism (Jachtenfuchs, Diez and Jung 1998; Eriksen and Fossum 2000; Warleigh 2002). Moreover, such a view of democracy tends to lay great emphasis on political participation, emphasizing community-building at the EU level as a result of sustained 'citizenship practice' (Wiener 1998; Bellamy 2001). Flexibility is thus at one level an issue of intergovernmentalism, or at least national government choice; but such choices can be reconciled with, or even partially produced by, popular will.

Thus, it is important to acknowledge that views of the democratic nature of flexibility ultimately depend on how democracy itself is considered to be constituted. Moreover, it is possible to view flexibility as part of a more democratic international order, albeit one which gives no centrality to the process of regional integration understood as state-building, rather than the defence of national sovereignty along communitarian lines. However, it is also necessary to acknowledge that the uses to which flexibility has been, or might be, put raise questions of democracy which are separate from those relating to flexibility's normative base. As a tool of policy making, flexibility is as susceptible to manipulation as any other instrument.

For example, although it is quite possible normatively to square flexibility with an increased role for the citizens—particularly since (*pace* Ehlermann 1998) they may be more likely to engage with a Union whose role is more in keeping with their general preferences about the scope and nature of transnational governance (Blondel, Sinnott and Svensson 1998)—it is quite another matter to ensure that the actual structures and decision-making processes of the Union are similarly elaborated. The Amsterdam Treaty stipulated that closer cooperation could not be allowed in cases where it would have a negative impact on the status of EU citizenship. However, the Nice Treaty removed this injunction, and replaced it with a far more general provision that CC must respect economic and social cohesion, which is both vaguer and more clearly focused on the state level than on the citizen (since it is primarily 'cohesion' between states, or perhaps regions, which the Treaty seeks to protect). Similarly, if the democratic status of flexibility is seen primarily as equality of opportunity and voice between member states, there is legitimate concern about whether the current fifteen states will extend this courtesy to those presently waiting to join. Tuytschaever (1999: 169) points out that to date the vast majority of opt-outs have been sought by the member state in question rather than imposed, and in addition closer cooperation is predicated on member state choice (with the 'neutral' Commission given a large role in determining whether a state which has opted out can later join). To take one example, however, Austro-German concerns about freedom of movement of labour look likely to deny citizens of Poland and other candidate states their full EU citizenship rights for a fairly long period, a decision which has even attracted much support in the EP (*European Voice*, 5–11 October 2000). It is thus by no means certain that flexibility will not be a device by which, to paraphrase Orwell, some member states and citizens are more equal than others—at least for a time.[8]

Furthermore, it is necessary to acknowledge that flexibility also asks difficult questions of the EU's institutional system. Although these

8. Of course, there is a precedent here in the cases of Portuguese and Spanish entry into the EU. Such arrangements are common as part of the accession phase; but in a context now shaped by the existence of EU citizenship as a formal set of rights and entitlements, these derogations take on a different nature, constituting a degree of exclusion from the political system rather than simply from the labour market.

problems can be exaggerated, it is nonetheless true that even for its normative advocates flexibility may involve a trade-off between worthy underlying principles and reductions to transparency (and, possibly, accountability)—especially since there is no guarantee that closer cooperation will be developed wholly in keeping with clearly inclusive normative principles. There are also problems of political representation. De la Serre and Wallace (1997) question whether it is justified to incorporate into the *acquis* measures which were initially decided by a sub-group of member states, especially when a state's non-participation was a consequence of incapacity rather than choice. For example, the incorporation of the Schengen agreement on freedom of movement into the Amsterdam Treaty gave it the full force of EC law, and yet Ireland has had no formal role in its development since it has been obliged to follow the UK's opt-out by a prior bilateral agreement (FitzGerald, Gillespie and Fanning 1996: 20). It is true that the Irish opt-out means that Schengen legislation does not automatically apply to it, and that nothing prevents Ireland 'opting in' in piecemeal fashion as the UK appears to be doing. Ireland could also have vetoed the incorporation of Schengen at the 1997 intergovernmental conference (IGC). However, this case is an example of how flexibility can be involuntary, and how a vanguard group may shape policy without the participation of member states which might wish to participate, but are prevented even if they neither oppose the measure in principle nor suffer from incapacity to implement it.

Representation is problematized by flexibility in other ways too (Neunreither 2000). Since flexibility implies issue-specific patterns of institutional participants, it also implies that the issue at hand is more important than the uniform empowerment of each institution. This could be particularly difficult for the Parliament to accept, since it is still effectively kept out of pillars 2 and 3, and still struggling to ensure that codecision is applied across the board in pillar 1. It must also be decided whether members of the European Parliament (MEPs) and Commissioners from member states which are not participating in a given policy regime should have the right to fulfil their institutional roles regarding that regime: should, for example, a social policy Commissioner from the UK be able to play the lead role for the Commission if the UK has opted out? Should MEPs from the UK retain their votes in the relevant Parliament committees and plenary? Here, as stated above, the solution appears to be an unofficial division of Union institutions into 'collegiate' (i.e. indivisible) and 'non-collegiate' (divisible) categories for the sake of closer cooperation (Neunreither 2000: 139). It would be well to formalize such arrangements, however, not least because EU citizenship gives nationals of one member state who reside in another the franchise for local and European elections: it is difficult to see why, for example, a Finn voting in Denmark for an MEP should be deprived of her representative voice on issues she may consider important merely because Copenhagen opts out—particularly if Helsinki opts in.

However, even in its under-determined guise as closer cooperation, flexibility is not without applications which favour democracy, or at least demonstrate that the two do not have to be in opposition—thus, flexibility is not a good normative idea whose translation into 'real-world politics' is necessarily questionable on democratic grounds. Von Weizsäcker, Dehaene and Simon (1999) point out that whatever the shortcomings of closer cooperation, bi- or multilateral cooperation by member states outside the Treaty framework is not subject to any of the oversight functions or checks and balances contained in EC law and the Union institutional system. Thus, at a very basic level, maintaining closer cooperation as part of the EU 'toolkit' may be a means of increasing the degree of democratic control of decision making even if it is not perfect. Furthermore, the Amsterdam Treaty amended the Treaty on European Union (established at Maastricht) to allow the suspension of voting rights in Council of any member state which is deemed by the others not to meet required standards of human rights protection. This is clearly different from matters of 'ordinary' closer cooperation; however, it does imply that even in the Treaty there are elements of cosmopolitanism invoked as the justification for differentiation (and thus flexibility).

Furthermore, flexibility is in keeping with the views of certain actors from 'below' the nation-state level who seek to use the integration process as a means of articulating sub-national identities (Keating 1999; MacCormick 1999). This does not mean that flexibility automatically or even elliptically leads towards a 'Europe of the Regions'; the halcyon period of advocates of the latter may well have passed (Jeffery 2000). However, it does mean that the Union can provide an arena for the resolution of tensions between state nationalisms and those of 'stateless nations' such as the Catalans, Basques and Scots (Keating 1999). This is because flexibility signals that the EU is not itself a (Westphalian) state-in-waiting; by promotion of diffuse and asymmetrical structures of governance, the EU could further separate nationality from citizenship rights (and vice versa), thereby allowing the articulation of overlapping political identities and adding a dimension of multi-level democracy to its existing multi-level governance.

Thus, perhaps the best way to summarize the problems of flexibility —be they systemic, policy style, external coherence, legal or democratic issues—is, as indicated in the introduction to this chapter and illustrated throughout it, that they reveal the need for a different kind of thinking about European integration, both strategically and normatively. Flexibility certainly undermines the case of those who see integration as a process of state-building, even though it is perfectly reconcilable with the federation of a sub-group of member states. Indeed, if closer cooperation is further reformed, it could be the mechanism which allows this to happen.

This is not to say that all the difficulties of flexibility can be transformed into advantages if we simply change the conceptual lens through which they are viewed. There is no simple cure for the difficulties of either European integration or flexibility. However, in order to ensure that flexibility is reformed and deployed to something like optimal effect, it is necessary to effect a shift in the way it is often approached in both academic and practitioner communities. Flexibility is too often considered a second best solution by proponents of the integration process, something to be fallen back on when all else fails. Even the Treaty currently regards it as a measure of last resort. (However, it is a moot point how far Commission officials and member governments who are determined to press ahead with a proposal, if necessary without the participation of all member states, would really go to explore all other avenues. In all likelihood they would take soundings from likely non-participant member states about whether they would object to the launch of a closer cooperation measure, and proceed on receipt of a positive reply.) Change must thus be effectuated in order to ensure that flexibility is considered a valid first-choice mode of integration rather than one into which actors are forced by circumstance.

This will not be an easy step. Putting forward her view of how ideational 'frames' (or conceptual predispositions) affect the integration process, Beate Kohler-Koch (2000) shows how important these 'frames' are to actors as a means of making sense of complex, ambiguous and evolving processes like European integration.[9] In other words, frames help actors interpret a given situation, and also to make decisions about what—if anything—can or should be done about it. However, frames can be a barrier to innovation, since those which have links with 'internalized categories of traditional thinking' are more likely to be successful than those which are wholly new—they represent less of a break with the past, and require less of a conceptual leap (Kohler-Koch 2000: 517). However, closer cooperation demonstrates the extent to which the practice of European integration has outpaced mainstream ability to 'frame' it successfully through orthodox approaches, meaning that many prescriptions for EU reform from both pro- and anti-integration perspectives are ill-founded and the EU continues to muddle through without a clear strategy. We are in the process of exchanging old frames for new, a process of debate and gradual change. Thus, what is needed is an articulation of flexibility which stresses how it can help deliver the main benefits of European integration while avoiding many of its most worrying features for defenders of national sovereignty. Such is the goal of the next, and final, chapter.

9.   See also the work of sociological institutionalists, as helpfully summarized in Hall and Taylor 1996.

5 |

Making Flexibility Work

Introduction

In this chapter I argue that flexibility can only be made to work satis-
factorily if a kind of à la carte model is applied to the integration process. In order to do this, I initially summarize the principal arguments
of the book so far, and return to the three models of flexibility set out in
Chapter 1 in order to assess their viability as models for reform of the
Union which are capable of solving the problems with flexibility identified in Chapter 4. I focus first on multi-speed and concentric circles
models before turning to the à la carte variant, and conclude the chapter
by setting out a working model of flexible European governance.

By way of introduction, then, it is worthwhile to review key aspects
of the preceding chapters of this book and show how they inform its
conclusion. In Chapter 1, I set out the reasons for the development of
flexibility in the EU, explaining how it has become such a prominent
feature of Union governance and the benefits it brings to that process
(chiefly, an improved capacity to manage diversity, facilitate further
enlargement, increase the success of day-to-day policy making, and
contribute to the resolution of the problem of the democratic deficit). I
also offered a typology of flexibility which divides it into multi-speed,
concentric circles and à la carte models. I also explained how each of
these models considers flexibility to arise, and what kind of vision of
the EU is inherent in each. To recap: multi-speed models consider
differentiation between member states to be dictated by incapacity of
certain states to implement a policy at the time of its general launch,
and envisages their eventual willing implementation of the full *acquis*
as soon as they are able. Concentric circles models divide the member
states into more or less permanent categories, in which national
governments decide just how much of the *acquis* they are able (or
perhaps willing) to accept, and in which certain member states are able
to constitute a clear vanguard group. À la carte models also envisage

the possibility of permanent division, but do so on a more particular basis, that is, opting out by individual policy rather than according to a predetermined package pertinent to membership of a given 'division' of the Union. Thus, the key differences between the models are the extent of member state choice they allow, and their attitude towards differentiation over the long term.

In Chapter 1, I also argued that the evolution of flexibility has been ambiguous and cautious, dictated by a contested process of European integration which the member states have sought to deepen in order to realize their (often at variance) individual and collective interests. This is a vital link to Chapter 2, which set out the best means to theorize flexibility, arguing that its best 'frame', in terms of both normative and explanatory processes, is a revised kind of functionalism. In Chapter 3, I set out in more detail how flexibility has actually been implemented in the Union so far, examining the development of 'closer cooperation' between the Amsterdam and Nice Treaties, tracing its 'constitutional-ization' at Amsterdam and its partial facilitation at Nice. Its remaining problems were discussed in depth in Chapter 4, in which I argued that issues raised by closer cooperation for Union policy style, EC law, democracy, and external policy are in essence the result of flexibility's continuing under-determination. Thus, in the present chapter I present a schema for the successful operation of flexibility which seeks to make good this crucial shortcoming.

Towards which Model of Flexibility?

The EU has yet to decide which model of flexibility it wants to adopt, and has developed closer cooperation in a way which simultaneously reflects aspects of all three variants. This has led to confusion, or at least ambiguity, in the academic debate as well as the practice of Union governance; for example, Junge (1999) maintains that à la carte inte-gration was ruled out by the Amsterdam Treaty, while Tuytschaever (1999; 2000) argues that it is this model which emerged from the same treaty as the most dominant, at least in instances of 'case-by-case and predetermined flexibility' (Tuytschaever 2000: 170). The following table is reproduced from Chapter 1 to demonstrate this more clearly.

Flexible Integration

Table 5.1: Closer Co-operation and Models of Flexibility

Variable	What the treaty says[a]	Corresponding model
Triggering mechanism	Varies according to pillar	Multi-speed (pillar 1); à la carte (pillars 2 and 3)
Quorum	Eight member states (not a majority)	Concentric circles
National veto over launch?	No (except in pillar 2)	À la carte
Present in all pillars?	Yes (but limited in pillar 2)	Concentric circles
Uniform across all pillars?	No	À la carte
A means to add new competences to the EU?	No	Multi-speed
Can laggards join the vanguard?	Yes	Multi-speed

a. In this table I refer to the *acquis* as it would stand after ratification of the Nice Treaty (still pending ratification at time of writing).

In fact, there is general agreement that if flexibility's purpose is to facilitate institutional reform, this hybrid genesis of closer cooperation is insufficient. For example, although writing before the Nice Treaty, Chaltiel (1998) argues that flexibility should be a 'defence' against à la carte integration and be a part of, not a substitute for, broader institutional reform—tasks for which it is inadequate because it is unclearly elaborated.[1] Shaw (1998) argues that the normative and managerial purposes of closer cooperation have been blurred, partly by the choice of this term as a label for flexibility and also because it remains insufficiently articulated as a constitutional principle.[2] Before exploring an appropriate solution to this problem, however, it is helpful to recall the kind of EU envisaged in each model of flexibility.

1.   It should be noted that Chaltiel does not argue for the same kind of flexible Europe as advocated in this book.

2.   Again, this pre-Nice judgment remains valid thereafter, given the continuing (albeit adapted) confusion in the elaboration of closer cooperation.

A Multi-speed Europe

This version of flexible European integration retains the maximum similarity with the integration process so far. This is because flexibility can in this configuration only be used as a means of meeting aims already agreed by all the member states, and must involve a majority of them. Those in the vanguard are committed to helping other member states catch up. All member states continue to have an obligation to accept the entire *acquis communautaire*, and are allowed to opt-out only temporarily on the grounds that technical capacity, rather than choice, is the basis of non-participation. Consequently, a multi-speed Europe is very similar to the traditional Community Method, albeit with a more overt and probably more frequent use of derogations from particular policies. However, multi-speed models do not allow member states to opt-out through choice rather than incapacity—if a member state is capable of implementing a measure on its launch, it must do so, and if not, it must make every effort to gain the necessary capacity in as short a time as possible. Thus, in a multi-speed Europe, the UK, Denmark and Sweden would have no right to remain outside the single currency and no member state could negotiate a similar opt-out in future.

This model envisages an EU which is highly differentiated, with member states located at various stages in the process of implementing Union policy in different areas at any given time, although eventually each individual piece of legislation is destined for across-the-board application. Because this model seeks ultimate uniformity and rests on solidarity between member states, it has long been the favoured option of many advocates of deeper European integration. It would produce a Union in which all member states agree to commit to a common *finalité politique*, even if that were unable to satisfy anyone, being too 'federal' for the preferences of some and too 'national' for others.

A Europe of Concentric Circles

In this model, the EU becomes divided into at least two clear divisions of membership, with national governments obliged explicitly to decide which tier they wish to join. Membership of each tier involves accepting a given package of obligations, but no more. This makes the EU relatively easy to manage, since its primary lines of division become clear and fairly permanent rather than complex and subject to change as they are now. Those in the first tier constitute a 'hard core', which agrees to accept all the *acquis* and pushes towards federalism. There is no requirement that this hard core must comprise a majority of member states. Those in the outer tiers accept varying degrees of European integration, either because they are incapable of accepting greater obligations or because they choose not to. With key decisions reserved for the hard core, it becomes more difficult for those outside to gain 'promotion' over time, since the volume of legislation to implement increases and those opting-out through incapacity are likely to fall further behind, while those opting out through choice are faced with the ever more daunting task of adopting structures, laws and policies which they did not shape. Thus, concentric circles models advocate a clear and quasi-permanent division of the Union into key member states and also-rans.

Because it advocates deeper integration for those member states which both wish for and are capable of it, and the consignment of all others to the periphery, it has often been advocated by some of the more powerful member states seeking to revitalize their influence in the EU by making explicit their role as the essential elite in the process—especially politicians in France and Germany (Lamers 1997, see also current French plans for a 'pioneer group'[3]). This is reflected in the current provision for flexibility measures to be launched by eight member states rather than a majority of them, although the number of states involved would still be quite high (and indeed, until further enlargement, would actually constitute a majority). Informally, something approaching a hard core might be said to consist already of those member states which are part of the Eurozone, implement the entire Schengen *acquis*, and are set to participate fully in the RRF, that is, France, Germany, Italy, Spain, Belgium, the Netherlands, Luxembourg, Portugal and Greece. However, it should be remembered that this is neither an official core nor a closed one, since the RRF is open to member states outside the Eurozone (e.g. the UK) and even to states which have yet to join the Union at all (e.g. Turkey, Poland, Hungary, the Czech Republic). Should this model of flexibility be adopted in full, the hard core would in all likelihood involve fewer member states.

An à la Carte Europe

This model is the most flexible of all in that it envisages the likelihood of permanent differentiation in EU membership, not according to which

---

3. See President Chirac's speech to the German *Bundestag* on 27 June 2000.

pre-set package of the *acquis* a member state is willing/able to accept but according to member state choice between different policy areas and even inside them. Thus, a member state could adopt the entire EMU *acquis* but sit out of the RRF as a result of its neutrality. Within environment policy, a member state with no coastline could, for example, opt-out of directives on maritime pollution but press hard for stringent legislation on clean air. This model would produce a compli-cated EU system with no formal core and different degrees of commit-ment from the member states, even within policy areas. It would not promote a common end-product of the integration process; neither would it seek to prevent such an outcome, but it would consider such a development most unlikely and rather seek to enable member states to cooperate with as many of their partners as possible, when possible. Because of this, and the attendant failure to emphasize across-the-board solidarity between the member states, the à la carte model has often been associated with those member states which seek to minimize their role in the integration process. However, it is implicit in three current characteristics of closer cooperation. First, the triggering mechanism, since in pillars 2 and 3 there are different likely core groups. Second, the lack of a national veto to prevent the launch of a CC measure in pillar 1 (which means that no member state can unilaterally impede progress). Third, the variation between the forms of CC in the different pillars, which implies the eventual creation of overlapping subsets of participating states rather than a clear division between them, an outcome also inherent in the absence of the veto in pillars 1 and 3.

The Orthodox Approaches: Multi-speed and Concentric Circle Models

There are several shortcomings in the multi-speed and concentric circles models of flexibility which rule them out as bases for the refinement of closer cooperation. As will be clear, however, they are vastly different. Multi-speed models tend to be distrustful of differen-tiation, and seek to both minimize it and organize it within very tightly policed and time-bound limits (Maillet and Vélo 1994). Concentric circles models seek to impose clear and enduring boundaries between the (groups of) member states, and privilege the most powerful over the weakest, however inexplicitly.

Moreover, multi-speed models completely fail to address the under-lying logic of the drive for flexibility: the existence of difference. Granting temporary derogations from particular policies (or, more likely, particular directives) is no substitute for tackling the issue of choice which may lie behind the request for a derogation. If an ideo-logical or otherwise political motivation shapes requests for flexibility, temporary arrangements grounded on an assessment of technical incap-acity are unlikely to satisfy either the member state requesting an opt-out or its partners. Although derogations based on such assessments can last for many years, such a state of affairs is fundamentally dishonest since in those cases the member state in question often has no intention of joining the mainstream (de la Serre and Wallace 1997). Instead of acknowledging difference, a façade of unity is erected while underneath differentiation can be extensive. Thus, multi-speed integration can be entirely without transparency, coping with difference only tacitly and incompletely.

Multi-speed models are predicated on the assumption that it is possible and desirable to devise *a priori* a set of core policies which must be adopted uniformly by all member states as the price of membership and which can be separated from those where flexibility is possible (for example, Duff 1997a: 15; Dewatripont *et al.* 1995). In the first, compulsory, group of policies, no flexibility is possible; in the second, temporary derogations are possible, but again this is based on capacity rather than choice. Such models are untenable on two grounds: the impossibility of defining core areas, and the assumption that all member states will wish to adopt all policies eventually (either through genuine will, or through need to catch up with the vanguard countries in order to share the benefits of their cooperation—a kind of reluctant acknowledgment of spillover).

On the first of these issues, it is entirely unclear that an integral set of policies can be defined. Such a core would presumably include the single market and currency; yet de Búrca (2000) shows the former has been subject to flexibility, even if all member states accept and support it in general. The euro is notorious in its failure to extend across the entire Union; member states are as likely to differ in their assessment of the acceptability of core policies as any other, indeed perhaps more so since they are closer to the heart of the integration project. Moreover, even in its application to twelve of the current member states, the single currency has required flexibility, in that Greece was unable to join initially due to a failure to meet the requisite convergence criteria.

The second issue raises a related point: it is by no means clear that opt-outs are dictated purely by technical incapacity rather than choice (see above), or even that when it is the crucial variable, capacity is capable of improvement in the short term. Derogations from aspects of the Common Agricultural Policy granted to Portugal and Spain took fifteen years to elapse; it is likely that countries from Central and Eastern Europe will require similar derogations from a greater number of policy areas, especially since the kind of financial support granted to the Iberian countries is likely to be denied those of the former Soviet bloc unless current trends in budget and policy reform are reversed. Multi-speed models consider that countries which opt-out really want to opt in, but are temporarily incapable of so doing; it also assumes that those member states which want to proceed will be willing to nurture them and foster their capacities until full participation is possible (Tindemans 1976). The history of the EU to date indicates that this is a naïve assumption on both scores.

Perhaps the most advanced kind of multi-speed integration is that elaborated by Dewatripont *et al.* (1995), whose scheme envisages the division of the *acquis* into two sections: core policies, which would need to be accepted by all member states in their entirety, and those in which flexibility would be possible. Although it does not share all the features of multi-speed integration, this scheme fits that model more closely than either of the others since it involves neither clear divisions of membership nor a totally free choice of which policies to adopt, but instead a uniform core complemented by a series of 'open partnerships' available to, but not compulsory for, all member states. In this scheme, two different institutional patterns are applied: the core policies are governed federally via a bicameral legislature, and the 'open partnerships' are governed intergovernmentally, under the auspices of a monitoring agency (ultimately under the European Council) empowered to ensure such partnerships do not conflict too sharply with the general *acquis*.

The great merit of this scheme is its attempt to accept what may be permanent differences grounded in choice rather than capacity, in the form of 'open partnerships'. However, it also contains several problems which undermine its coherence. First, the open partnerships are envisaged to be both intergovernmental and less integrated than the core policies, neither of which would necessarily be the case in reality:

flexibility is often chosen to allow integration to proceed more quickly and/or more deeply than would otherwise be the case. Second, the institutional design of non-core policy regimes would be subject to input from member states which decide not to participate in them. This might avoid 'discrimination' against non-participants, but it is also likely to allow the latter to free ride even if they do not seek to place restrictions on the capacities of the 'open partnership'. Third, 'open partnerships' would be likely to cause rivalry between the institutions of the core policies and those of the sectoral regimes, from which 'core policy' institutions would be explicitly barred. The first two problems point towards a desire to privilege uniformity rather than flexibility, and thus an incomplete acceptance of difference; the third indicates a potential for conflict which would make that uniformity less likely. Thus, even in reformed models, multi-speed integration is unsuited to the key tasks of flexibility.

Concentric circles models are even more clearly inadequate. Less idealistic than their multi-speed equivalents, they assume different national capacities for, and views of, integration to be essentially permanent. Thus, they should be acknowledged if those states which can benefit most from integration are to be enabled to pursue it optimally (Lamers 1997). This perspective contains an element of truth, but the advocacy in these models of several discrete tiers of membership around a hard core of both states and policies fails to allow adequately for changes in either choice or capacity over time. For example, the 1997 general election in the UK brought to power a government which reversed its predecessor's decision to opt out of the social charter—but which did not accept EU social policy in its entirety, and which continues to stay outside the single currency. If the EU had been a system of concentric circles, such partial opt-ins would have been impossible, since it would be necessary to accept entire policies rather than parts of them; moreover, since social policy is a likely candidate for inclusion in the hard core of policy areas, it is unlikely that the UK could have made such a reversal while remaining outside the euro and much of the Schengen *acquis*.

Such models contain two further crucial flaws. First, if it is difficult to separate core and other policies into two discrete sections, it is likely to be even more problematic to create three or more such categories. Second, by conflating capacity with choice concentric circles models confine to the periphery those member states which might be willing to participate in certain policies but which are presently (and possibly temporarily) incapable of so doing. With a view to further enlargement, a Europe of concentric circles would in all likelihood mean that those states currently in the queue to join the Union would find themselves second, third or fourth tier members for a considerable period of time. This would be both undemocratic and unable to reflect the reality of such states' differentiated capacities to contribute to and participate in the development of the Union: for example, as members of NATO, the contribution of Poland, Hungary and the Czech Republic to most if not all decisions of the second pillar will be vital immediately on their entry to the Union, even if their ability to join the single currency is open to question in even the medium term. Thus, both orthodox models of flexibility are unsuitable for the EU, although their ability to fit the interests of certain key players (for multi-speed, the Commission, Parliament and more federally minded member states; for concentric circles, certain German politicians and many in the French elite) has enabled them to shape the elaboration of closer cooperation to date.

The Unorthodox Approach: An à la Carte Europe

The third model of flexibility, however, is more promising, because it allows for continual difference between member states' capacity and will to participate on an issue-by-issue basis, even within a policy area. It neither assumes all member states seek essentially the same goal nor rules that out; it neither consigns certain member states to the periphery by defining as core issues policy areas which they are unable or unwilling to adopt, nor does it rule out the unofficial leadership of the integration process by those member states which are willing to commit most to it. However, it is grounded in certain normative assumptions which must be acknowledged if it is to be adopted successfully. It also considers that significant differentiation may be a permanent feature of European integration, even if the specific form of that differentiation is likely to be both complex and subject to change over time. Such assumptions are difficult to reconcile with the traditional community method, and also with plans to make the Union subject to the joint rule of a collective hegemon in the form of a hard core.

The first objection levelled against à la carte integration is that it would permit excessive diversity in the integration process, creating a Union which would be impossible to manage effectively and offering the simultaneous ability to undermine the achievements of the EU to date. This is inaccurate. First, the treaty already forbids the use of flexibility to unravel the existing *acquis*, an obligation which is commensurable with à la carte models even if the twin injunction—that flexibility may not be used to add to the *acquis*—is not (see below). Second, even if the treaty contained no such measure, it is unlikely that member states which have invested so heavily (in both political and economic terms) in the single market and currency would suddenly seek to opt out of both, and thereby get no return from their freely chosen but often painful commitments. Third, while the degree of complexity introduced by flexibility could well be great, this presents managerial challenges rather than Herculean labours (Stubb 1997); given the political will, there is no *a priori* reason why such a system could not be run effectively. Member states are far more likely to grant the necessary administrative and decision capacities to the Union if their involvement is more readily commensurable with perceived national interests. As Scharpf (1999) indicates, existing experiments with this kind of flexible integration such as the UK and Danish opt-outs from EMU have given it greater respectability than in the past— the policy regime in question has survived to the general benefit of its participant states (despite difficulties with the international financial markets), and neither the UK nor Denmark appears to consider itself of lesser status than those member states in the Eurozone.

Moreover, since it sees no policy regime to be necessarily the preserve of any group of member states, only the à la carte model of flexibility allows member states potentially to add to the entire *acquis* while also permitting them to cooperate bi- or multi-laterally outside it. It acknowledges that in a Europe of multiple governance regimes, extra-EU cooperation is often necessary and that the EU is itself one of those interlocking regimes. It also ensures that such cooperation is likely to be a complement rather than a rival to the EU by making collaboration within the Union structures more attractive (since it would be freely chosen), and less onerous (for the same reason). Thus, the à la carte model means that flexibility can allow member states to progress their collaborations in multiple arenas, and would not be frustrated by an equivalent of the current restrictions placed on closer cooperation.

However, the corollary of this is the acceptance of the normative 'frame' of à la carte flexibility, and choosing to consider it worthwhile in its own right rather than an expedient tool for diversity management which should ultimately be discarded. As argued by Shaw (2000: 338), flexibility pushes integration towards 'dialogic and procedural constitutionalism, including a duty to negotiate and...tolerance of partial, fragmented and interim outcomes, formulated in the knowledge that the dialogue will continue'. Thus, it points towards asymmetrical outcomes which are themselves considered liable to change as part of an ongoing process—the kind of organic development advocated by the functionalists (Mitrany 1933; 1944—see Chapter 2). Smith (2000) maintains that by ensuring the EU has no clear hierarchy in many aspects of its current configuration, member states have made certain (either deliberately or not) that this kind of negotiation has already become a key feature of the system. Hierarchical structures with clear boundaries and responsibilities favour competitive bargaining and their own maintenance; multi-layer, network-dominated systems such as the EU, on the other hand, vary in both the scope and the scale of authority. They are thus predisposed towards negotiation about the balance of and relationship between the different layers, and also about the best ways to solve problems, since the system requires actors to improve their knowledge of each other.

The EU system's reinforcement comes through its utility in fulfilling this problem-solving, transaction cost-reducing function (Smith 2000). The community method is now supplanted or at least accompanied by other forms of decision making (Wallace 2000b); the Maastricht Treaty heralded an explicit decision that deepening integration required greater differentiation in terms of both structure of the Union and levels of member state participation, a choice subsequently if incompletely articulated in the provisions on closer cooperation. In other words, the practice of governance in the EU has been brought into line with many of those attached to the à la carte model, but its structures and 'frame' have not. Thus, further (and overt) reform to both institutions and ethos of the Union is necessary.

It is precisely this kind of change which may be hardest to make. The elitist, and more or less explicitly state-forming (albeit welfare-oriented) 'ethics of integration' (Bellamy and Warleigh 1998) continues to inform the views about the future of the Union of many key actors—both in favour of and against further deepening. As shown by scholars writing at different stages in the integration process, à la carte integration has often been deliberately and erroneously constructed as coterminous with intergovernmentalism by those with an institutional interest in federalizing the Union (on this elision, see Taylor 1983; Wind 1998; Tuytschaever 1999; Philippart and Sie Dian Ho 2000). This process has contemporary echoes in the conservative new orthodoxy clustering around multi-speed models, indicating that, steeped in outdated norms, the very institutional proactivism sought by the original architects of European integration may contribute to the latter's stagnation if it goes unchanged by such processes as the post-Nice dialogue. This must be borne in mind when considering the blueprint for the operationalization of flexibility set out below.

Towards a Blueprint for Flexible European Integration

The purpose of this blueprint is to act as a basis upon which flexibility could be more successfully operationalized than at present, but it is also envisaged as part of the ongoing evolution of the EU itself—thus, it is not presented as an end product, but rather as work in progress. However, even such a conditional blueprint is necessary in order to understand how flexibility may be harnessed in a way which adds to the prospects for deeper and more successful European integration, bridging the gap between increased instrumental recourse to flexibility and, as the Treaty currently stands, its unclear normative rationale. Such a blueprint is also necessary to inform the process of dialogue and evolution identified above, so that the informal use of flexibility in order to avoid decisions about its true implications and nature, a concern raised by Shaw (1998), is minimized. Flexibility obliges member states to decide just how much European integration they wish to support and engage with; this blueprint may play a role in ensuring that such choices are explicit. However, as with all such blueprints it is open to charges of incompleteness, naïvety and/or idealism—so it should be understood that it is intended as a departure point for debate rather than an explanation or prediction of the ongoing process of Union reform. As such it has the merit of putting forward an alternative 'frame' for European integration, one which is at least potentially brought nearer to the light of day by the still-unresolved issue of flexibility. It is informed by functionalist principles, but it is by no means the only way in which the latter could be applied to the case of the EU.

A functionalist-flexible EU would be one in which 'essential contestation' (Bañkowski and Scott 1998) is prized, and in which a sense of common political identity and mutual dependence is gradually fostered at both elite and mass levels—as far as is possible—through the resolution via dialogue of conflict between different principles and norms, and in which remaining differences are treated as legitimate rather than perverse.

Since the objective of European integration would be ensuring peace and prosperity across the continent in a context of complex interdependence rather than the creation of a closed regional power bloc, membership of individual EU policy regimes would be open in principle to any European country as well as the current member states. Membership of the EU as a whole would require a contribution to the general budget and agreement to adopt all the Union *acquis* presently on the statute book and not subject to explicit opt-out. Thus, for example, it would be necessary to adopt general provisions of environment policy, but not necessarily the single currency. Membership would confer in return the right to representation in all the institutions of the EU, and consequently an ability to shape treaty reform. Thus, the EU would become a more truly cosmopolitan enterprise. In this respect, the Rapid Reaction Force, which functions as part of the transatlantic security regime and is open to participation from non-EU states while certain member states opt out is a useful, if imperfect, model.

Choice would become the key principle of participation in the Union. Those member states with continuing preferences to opt out of large sections of the integration project would be less truculent about taking part in the process as a whole, since they could tailor their participation to suit their interests (however perceived). States outside the Union and seeking to join it, but with protracted problems of capacity, would have two potential sources of help. First, over time, some improvement in their overall membership ability would be generated by participation in as much of the single market and other policy regimes as possible—a key advantage of functionalist-inspired flexibility which would go beyond the current practice of association agreements. Second, there could be a system of targeted loans provided by the European Bank for Reconstruction and Development (EBRD)—and thus funded indirectly by the member states—payable to help such states adapt to the requirements of specific policy regimes. Such loans would not be granted automatically, but would instead have to be applied for and approved by the EBRD. It would not in all likelihood be possible to extend the structural funds beyond their present limits, since this would

effectively mean asking member states to prepare others for membership of policy regimes they do not themselves support, but such an
initiative would be wholly in keeping with this kind of flexibility were
it to arise.[4]

As the price of entry into any and all policy regimes, member states
and those participants from outside the EU would pledge to respect
certain norms of (liberal) democratic governance, such as an independent judiciary and the rule of law. They would also subject themselves
to common principles such as respect for human rights and equal
opportunities. Those member states choosing not to participate in a
given Union policy regime would agree not to develop contradictory
policies at extra-EU level, an offence which would be justiciable before
the European Court of Justice. Contributions to the EU budget would
be of two kinds; a general contribution for which all member states
would be liable, and which would pay for the running of the EU institutions as well as the costs of any policies which happen to be adopted
by all member states. Each separate policy regime would be paid for
equally by participant states (including those from outside the Union, if
appropriate) by mechanisms determined nationally—possibly by explicit levy, possibly by funds earmarked for the purpose in the national
budget. The pillar structure would remain, albeit subject to change by
treaty reform (see below). Flexibility would, however, work in a similar
way in each pillar, since the capacity of each member state to opt out
would remove its need for a veto and ensure that principles held dear
(such as neutrality) are unaffected. Thus, integration would remain
somewhat organic but also become more profoundly political than it
has been so far, moving away from the primacy of economics as a
motor of integration.

The Union is envisaged as a set of overlapping, policy-specific
networks under a set of common institutions, none of which would be
divisible except for the Council, with member governments exercising
their power of choice to opt in or out of policy regimes at their launch
or, as noted above, upon joining the Union (in the case of policy areas
already part of the *acquis* and not subject to previous opt-outs). Within

---

4.   This is a clear indicator of lack of solidarity. However, the general lack of
will on the part of the current member states to contribute more money to the
structural funds—and the determination of states such as Spain to hold on to the
share of such money that they already receive—indicate that the EU will not acquire
a significantly greater role as a redistributor of resources in the foreseeable future.

each policy regime, Union institutions would be used, and policies made by the participant states would constitute the Union *acquis* in that policy area (building on the existing legislation if necessary). However it would be possible to set certain technical entry criteria where appropriate (such as for the euro), as defined in advance by the Council Secretariat. In such cases, states wishing to join a regime after its launch would have their suitability assessed against the criteria by the Council Secretariat and voted upon by the already participating states by simple majority. Rejections would be subject to appeal at the Court of Justice if the eligibility criteria appear objectively to have been met.

No part of the *acquis* would formally be put beyond the scope of flexibility. Once having chosen to participate in a given policy regime, however, all governments would have to abide by its rules and legislation or seek their reform on a multilateral basis, agreed to by all governments participating in the regime and, in pillar 1, by the relevant committee of the European Parliament. Opting out after participation in a regime would not allow member states to avoid commitments made while inside it, unless specific permission to do this were granted by those states which continue inside the regime. Each policy regime would be launched subject to attracting a quorum of member states in order to avoid joint hegemony by two or three governments, set at an initial level of five but subject to revision upon enlargement should that prove necessary.[5] States from outside the Union would be admitted to a regime by simple majority vote of the participant member states, but would have no say over the launch of a regime. If admitted, they would be entitled to representation at governmental level on an equal basis with participating member states (one state, one vote). They would not be entitled to seats in the European Parliament; this would be a privilege of membership of the Union. Within each policy regime, participant states would vote by simple majority.

External representation of the Union would be a task for the President of the European Parliament in most matters of the first pillar, with appropriate exceptions in favour of the President of the European Central Bank (ECB). The Secretary General of the Council would continue this function for pillars 2 and 3, as well as external trade negotiation such as in the WTO. The Presidency of the Council would be abolished, since it could not be guaranteed that any member state

5.   See below for a discussion of treaty change.

would participate in every policy regime. Instead, leadership and an ability to liaise between the various member and participant states—and policy regimes—would be supplied by the Secretary General, whose powers and functions would thus be extended. The Secretary General would be elected every four or five years by a simple majority of both member states and MEPs from a list supplied by the member states. She or he would have the ability to appoint a *cabinet* of advisers; both would ultimately be accountable to the European Council and the EP (in plenary), although in the first instance the Secretary General would clearly have the ability to hold her/his own staff to account. The Secretary General would also formally head a Council department responsible for liaising between member states in each policy regime and the relevant EP committee under codecision. COREPER I and II would function as venues for interstate negotiation between participants within each policy regime, but would ultimately be accountable to the Secretary General, at least as far as codecision is concerned. Non-member states participating in EU regimes would not be represented in COREPER.

Matters of treaty reform would be configured rather differently in this kind of Union, since it would be possible to add to the *acquis* at any time by gathering the support of a quorum (not a majority) of member states in the Council. The present practice of summits leading to new treaties could thus be used less often, perhaps principally at times of significant 'constitutional change', thereby further removing the need for a Council Presidency as currently constituted. Such summits would involve equal numbers of delegates from the member states and the European Parliament, under the leadership of the Secretary General of the Council. They would be triggered by a vote of a simple majority in the European Council.

The Court of Justice would be empowered to ensure that each policy regime follows the rule of (EC) law, and to resolve any relevant disputes between actors from different regimes. Access to the Court would be granted to individuals as well as member governments and institutions of the Union. The European Parliament would use its Rules of Procedure to empower its committees to play an even greater role, allowing the relevant committee the opportunity to act as if it were the entire EP in each policy sector, liaising with both the participant governments and their national parliaments as appropriate in matters of legislation, and with the ECB in matters of scrutinizing the running of the single currency. Co-decision is perfectly commensurable with this, especially in its simplified, post-Amsterdam form. Plenary votes in the EP would only be necessary for issues such as accession of new member states and the approval of treaty changes, the latter constituting an advance on current practice. The right of legislative initiative would pass to an enlarged and better-resourced Council Secretariat in consultation with the pertinent EP committee. The Economic and Social Committee and Committee of the Regions would become specialist think-tanks capable of drafting reports on policy matters to be addressed at Union level, which would be addressed to both Council and EP. They would be entitled to a reasoned opinion for rejection from the Council should the latter choose not to respond favourably, a right which would be fully justiciable before the ECJ. The ECB would continue essentially as at present, with increased oversight responsibilities granted to the EP's economic and monetary affairs committee. The Bank's treaty basis would be subject to change by a two-thirds majority of member states participating in the Eurozone.

The Commission would not feature in this flexible Union. Its tasks would be transferred to the other institutions (as indicated above), with the role of the day-to-day civil service of the Union being entrusted to the Council Secretariat (which would of course need further resources). This would have several benefits. The main tasks of the Commission—to initiate legislation, to act as 'Guardian of the Treaties', to act as mediator, to regulate, to represent the EU externally (Cini 2001)—have never sat easily together, since they fuse administrative and highly political functions. Moreover, the Commission has never been allowed to play the leadership role sought for it by Monnet—the Delors period being perhaps a limited exception (Cini 2001)—and its ongoing, half-hearted attempts to reform itself have so far led to disaster (the mass resignation of Commissioners in 1999), and reduced credibility. The White Paper on European Governance (CEC 2001) continues this trend; although it contains much which is of use, its primary function is to justify and reform the role of the Commission in the perceived interests of that institution, rather than to seek radical reform of the Union as a whole (Wincott 2001).

This situation is not entirely the Commission's fault; the member states have continued to load responsibilities upon it and refused to give it the requisite resources. The Commission continues to be a scapegoat, blamed by national governments for the shortcomings of the EU and yet instructed to reduce its ambitions for the Union and insufficiently reformed or resourced to do its job properly. Even the Commission has begun to acknowledge this publicly (CEC 2001). Integral to the Monnet method of integration, the Commission's principal job was to cultivate spillover until such time as the Union became a federal state. Maastricht indicated the point at which that method of integration was essentially if not explicitly rejected by the member states, and it is necessary for the structures of the EU to reflect this more accurately in order to deepen transparency. Abolition of the Commission would have further advantages. First, it would rule out the equation of the 'European' interest with that of one particular institution, since the EP and Council would have overall control of what are currently the Commission's tasks and responsibilities. This would mean that no institution could arrogate to itself sole responsibility for the 'European project' and thus develop the view that its interests were *ipso facto* those of the EU as a whole—a tendency often present in the Commission (Cram 1997). Second, it would mean that member (as well as participant) governments would be more clearly responsible for their choices. However, the Commission should only be abolished as part of a radical package of reform and not as a single intergovernmentalist gesture; unless accompanying reforms are also made, and other actors entrusted with its tasks (and more resources), the demise of the Commission would endanger the success of the integration process itself.

The member states have collectively produced a European Union with which no-one is truly satisfied, and whose deficiencies in legitimacy, problem-resolution capacity and leadership threaten to become chronic as well as severe. Moreover, the member states are not, as a bloc, prepared to make the necessary commitment and sacrifices required by the traditionally proposed solution: the creation of a United States of Europe. Thus, making flexibility work optimally requires institutional and normative reform of the Union on an impressive scale. It requires the explicit abandonment of the Community Method, a clear and rather different normative basis for the integration project, and the commitment of greater resources by the member states. All of this is, of course, highly controversial—even if by adopting such a plan member states will be able both to target their spending more clearly towards their own preferences and share the cost burden with participant states from outside the Union, thereby increasing the likelihood of a perceived *juste retour*.

The post-Nice process offers an opportunity for reform in which flexibility could play a major part. The elaboration of flexibility to date has been confused and excessively cautious, and illustrates the fact that seeking to marry it with the Community Method is a task with small prospects of success. Bolder and more imaginative thinking is thus necessary. In all likelihood, the next IGC in 2004 will not produce anything closely resembling the above blueprint. It is also unlikely to produce a 'final solution' to the problems of Union governance. However, as an officially sanctioned means of making the Union function more effectively, this process and the eventual summit which will be its culmination must address these deficiencies squarely. They must also address the fact that the different member states have often fundamentally different views about what the solutions to these problems can, or should, be. Flexibility is an asset which cannot be ignored in such a situation: it is surely no coincidence that the RRF, which will allow the Union to play a more constructive part in the security governance of the continent, has been established as a result, and as a new form, of flexibility. As the EU assumes a more important role in world affairs while facing greater internal diversity, it is likely to require such solutions with increasing frequency. The role of this book has been to show how this might be done most effectively, and with the greatest clarity.

Appendix 1

Treaty on European Union Provisions on Closer Cooperation, as Introduced by the Treaty of Amsterdam*

TITLE VII (ex Title VIa)

PROVISIONS ON CLOSER COOPERATION

Article 43 (ex Article K.15)

1.   Member States which intend to establish closer cooperation between themselves may make use of the institutions, procedures and mechanisms laid down by this Treaty and the Treaty establishing the European Community provided that the cooperation:

(a)   is aimed at furthering the objectives of the Union and at protecting and serving its interests;

(b)   respects the principles of the said Treaties and the single institutional framework of the Union;

(c)   is only used as a last resort, where the objectives of the said Treaties could not be attained by applying the relevant procedures laid down therein;

(d)   concerns at least a majority of Member States;

(e)   does not affect the 'acquis communautaire' and the measures adopted under the other provisions of the said Treaties;

(f)   does not affect the competences, rights, obligations and interests of those Member States which do not participate therein;

(g)   is open to all Member States and allows them to become parties to the cooperation at any time, provided that they comply with the basic decision and with the decisions taken within that framework;

(h)   complies with the specific additional criteria laid down in Article 11 of the Treaty establishing the European Community and Article 40 of this Treaty, depending on the area concerned, and is authorised by the Council in accordance with the procedures laid down therein.

*   *Source*: Consolidated Version of the Treaty on European Union. The full text of this treaty is available at: http://europa.eu.int/eur-lex/en/treaties/index.html

2.   Member States shall apply, as far as they are concerned, the acts and decisions adopted for the implementation of the cooperation in which they participate. Member States not participating in such cooperation shall not impede the implementation thereof by the participating Member States.

Article 44 (ex Article K.16)

1.   For the purposes of the adoption of the acts and decisions necessary for the implementation of the cooperation referred to in Article 43, the relevant institutional provisions of this Treaty and of the Treaty establishing the European Community shall apply. However, while all members of the Council shall be able to take part in the deliberations, only those representing participating Member States shall take part in the adoption of decisions. The qualified majority shall be defined as the same proportion of the weighted votes of the members of the Council concerned as laid down in Article 205(2) of the Treaty establishing the European Community. Unanimity shall be constituted by only those Council members concerned.

2.   Expenditure resulting from implementation of the cooperation, other than administrative costs entailed for the institutions, shall be borne by the participating Member States, unless the Council, acting unanimously, decides otherwise.

Article 45 (ex Article K.17)

The Council and the Commission shall regularly inform the European Parliament of the development of closer cooperation established on the basis of this Title.

TITLE VIII (ex Title VII)

FINAL PROVISIONS

Article 46 (ex Article L)

The provisions of the Treaty establishing the European Community, the Treaty establishing the European Coal and Steel Community and the Treaty establishing the European Atomic Energy Community concerning the powers of the Court of justice of the European Communities and the exercise of those powers shall apply only to the following provisions of this Treaty:

(a)   provisions amending the Treaty establishing the European Economic Community with a view to establishing the European Community, the Treaty establishing the European Coal and Steel Community and the Treaty establishing the European Atomic Energy Community;

(b)   provisions of Title VI, under the conditions provided for by Article 35;

(c)   provisions of Title VII, under the conditions provided for by Article 11 of the Treaty establishing the European Community and Article 40 of this Treaty;

(d)   Article 6(2) with regard to action of the institutions, insofar as the Court has jurisdiction under the Treaties establishing the European Communities and under this Treaty;

(e)   Articles 46 to 53.

Article 47 (ex Article M)

Subject to the provisions amending the Treaty establishing the European Economic Community with a view to establishing the European Community, the Treaty establishing the European Coal and Steel Community and the Treaty establishing the European Atomic Energy Community, and to these final provisions, nothing in this Treaty shall affect the Treaties establishing the European Communities or the subsequent Treaties and Acts modifying or supplementing them.

Article 48 (ex Article N)

The government of any Member State or the Commission may submit to the Council proposals for the amendment of the Treaties on which the Union is founded.

If the Council, after consulting the European Parliament and, where appropriate, the Commission, delivers an opinion in favour of calling a conference of representatives of the governments of the Member States, the conference shall be convened by the President of the Council for the purpose of determining by common accord the amendments to be made to those Treaties. The European Central Bank shall also be consulted in the case of institutional changes in the monetary area.

The amendments shall enter into force after being ratified by all the Member States in accordance with their respective constitutional requirements.

Article 49 (ex Article 0)

Any European State which respects the principles set out in Article 6(1) may apply to become a member of the Union. It shall address its application to the Council, which shall act unanimously after consulting the Commission and after receiving the assent of the European Parliament, which shall act by an absolute majority of its component members.

The conditions of admission and the adjustments to the Treaties on which the Union is founded which such admission entails shall be the subject of an agreement between the Member States and the applicant State. This agreement shall be submitted for ratification by all the contracting States in accordance with their respective constitutional requirements.

Article 50 (ex Article P)

1.   Articles 2 to 7 and 10 to 19 of the Treaty establishing a Single Council and a Single Commission of the European Communities, signed in Brussels on 8 April 1965, are hereby repealed.

2.   Article 2, Article 3(2) and Title III of the Single European Act signed in Luxembourg on 17 February 1986 and in The Hague on 28 February 1986 are hereby repealed.

Article 51 (ex Article Q)

This Treaty is concluded for an unlimited period.

Article 52 (ex Article R)

1.   This Treaty shall be ratified by the High Contracting Parties in accordance with their respective constitutional requirements. The instruments of ratification shall be deposited with the Government of the Italian Republic.

2.   This Treaty shall enter into force on 1 January 1993, provided that all the instruments of ratification have been deposited, or, failing that, on the first day of the month following the deposit of the instrument of ratification by the last signatory State to take this step.

Article 53 (ex Article S)

This Treaty, drawn up in a single original in the Danish, Dutch, English, French, German, Greek, Irish, Italian, Portuguese and Spanish languages, the texts in each of these languages being equally authentic, shall be deposited in the archives of the government of the Italian Republic, which will transmit a certified copy to each of the governments of the other signatory States.

Pursuant to the Accession Treaty of 1994, the Finnish and Swedish versions of this Treaty shall also be authentic.

In witness whereof the undersigned Plenipotentiaries have signed this Treaty.

Done at Maastricht on the seventh day of February in the year one thousand nine hundred and ninety-two.

Mark EYSKENS   Philippe AIAYSTADT
Uffe ELLEMANN-JENSEN   Anders FOGH RASMUSSEN
Hans-Dictrich GENSCHER   Theodor WAIGEL
Antonios SANIARAS   Efthymios CHRISTODOULOU
Francisco FERNANDEZ ORDOREZ   Carlos SOLCHAGA CATALAN
Roland DUMAS   Pierre BEREGOVOY
Gerard COLLINS   Bertie AHERN
Gianni DE MICHELIS   Guido CARLI
Jacques F. POOS   Jean-Claude SUNCKER
Hans VAN DEN BROEK   Willem KOK
Joao de Deus PINHEIRO   Jorge BPAGA DE MACEDO
Douglas HURD   Francis MAUDE

Appendix 2

**Treaty Establishing the European Community Provisions on
Closer Cooperation, as Introduced by the Treaty of Amsterdam**[*]

Article 11 (ex Article 5a)

1.   Member States which intend to establish closer cooperation between themselves may be authorised, subject to Articles 43 and 44 of the Treaty on European
Union, to make use of the institutions, procedures and mechanisms laid down by
this Treaty, provided that the cooperation proposed:

   (a)   does not concern areas which fall within the exclusive competence of the
          Community;
   (b)   does not affect Community policies, actions or programmes;
   (c)   does not concern the citizenship of the Union or discriminate between
          nationals of Member States;
   (d)   remains within the limits of the powers conferred upon the Community
          by this Treaty; and
   (e)   does not constitute a discrimination or a restriction of trade between
          Member States and does not distort the conditions of competition
          between the latter.

2.   The authorisation referred to in paragraph 1 shall be granted by the Council,
acting by a qualified majority on a proposal from the Commission and after consulting the European Parliament.

If a member of the Council declares that, for important and stated reasons of
national policy, it intends to oppose the granting of an authorisation by qualified
majority, a vote shall not be taken. The Council may, acting by a qualified majority,
request that the matter be referred to the Council, meeting in the composition ot the
Heads of State or Government, for decision by unanimity.

*   *Source*: Consolidated Version of the Treaty Establishing the European
Community. The full text of this treaty is available at: http://europa.eu.int/eur-
lex/en/treaties/index.html

Member States which intend to establish closer cooperation as referred to in paragraph 1 may address a request to the Commission, which may submit a proposal to the Council to that effect. In the event of the Commission not submitting a proposal, it shall inform the Member States concerned of the reasons for not doing so.

3.   Any Member State which wishes to become a party to cooperation set up in accordance with this Article shall notify its intention to the Council and to the Commission, which shall give an opinion to the Council within three months of receipt of that notification. Within four months of the date of that notification, the Commission shall decide on it and on such specific arrangements as it may deem necessary.

4.   The acts and decisions necessary for the implementation of cooperation activities shall be subject to all the relevant provisions of this Treaty, save as otherwise provided for in this Article and in Articles 43 and 44 of the Treaty on European Union.

5.   This Article is without prejudice to the provisions of the Protocol integrating the Schengen acquis into the framework of the European Union.

Appendix 3

Draft Treaty of Nice Provisions on Closer Cooperation[*]

A) Provisions for the Common Foreign and Security Policy (Pillar 2)

6. The following Articles shall be inserted:

'Article 27a

1. Enhanced cooperation in any of the areas referred to in this Title shall be aimed at safeguarding the values and serving the interests of the Union as a whole by asserting its identity as a coherent force on the international scene. It shall respect:

–   the principles, objectives, general guidelines and consistency of the common foreign and security policy and the decisions taken within the framework of that policy;
–   the powers of the European Community, and
–   consistency between all the Union's policies and its external activities.

2. Articles 11 to 27 and Articles 27b to 28 shall apply to the enhanced cooperation provided for in this Article, save as otherwise provided in Article 27c and Articles 43 to 45.

Article 27b

Enhanced cooperation pursuant to this Title shall relate to implementation of a joint action or a common position. it shall not relate to matters having military or defence implications.

Article 27c

Member States which intend to establish enhanced cooperation between themselves under Article 27b shall address a request to the Council to that effect.

*   *Source*: Treaty of Nice (2001/C80/01). The full text of this treaty is available at: http://europa.eu.int/eur-lex/en/treaties/index.html

The request shall be forwarded to the Commission and to the European Parliament for information. The Commission shall give its opinion particularly on whether the enhanced cooperation proposed is consistent with Union policies. Authorisation shall be granted by the Council, acting in accordance with the second and third subparagraphs of Article 23(2) and in compliance with Articles 43 to 45.

Article 27d

Without prejudice to the powers of the Presidency or of the Commission, the Secretary-General of the Council, High Representative for the common foreign and security policy, shall in particular ensure that the European Parliament and all members of the Council are kept fully informed of the implementation of enhanced cooperation in the field of the common foreign and security policy.

Article 27e

Any Member State which wishes to participate in enhanced cooperation established in accordance with Article 27c shall notify its intention to the Council and inform the Commission. The Commission shall give an opinion to the Council within three months of the date of receipt of that notification. Within four months of the date of receipt of that notification, the Council shall take a decision on the request and on such specific arrangements as it may deem necessary. The decision shall be deemed to be taken unless the Council, acting by a qualified majority within the same period, decides to hold it in abeyance; in that case, the Council shall state the reasons for its decision and set a deadline for re-examining it.

For the purposes of this Article, the Council shall act by a qualified majority. The qualified majority shall be defined as the same proportion of the weighted votes and the same proportion of the number of the members of the Council concerned as those laid down in the third subparagraph of Article 23(2).'

7.   In Article 29, second paragraph, the second indent shall be replaced by the following:

'–   closer cooperation between judicial and other competent authorities of the Member States, including cooperation through the European Judicial Cooperation Unit ('Eurojust'), in accordance with the provisions of Articles 31 and 32:'

B) Provisions for Judicial Cooperation in Criminal Matters (Pillar 3)
Article 40 shall be replaced by the following Articles 40, 40a and 40b:

'Article 40

1.   Enhanced cooperation in any of the areas referred to in this Title shall have the aim of enabling the Union to develop more rapidly into an area of freedom, security

and justice, while respecting the powers of the European Community and the objectives laid down in this Title.

2.   Articles 29 to 39 and Articles 40a to 41 shall apply to the enhanced cooperation provided for by this Article, save as otherwise provided in Article 40a and in Articles 43 to 45.

3.   The provisions of the Treaty establishing the European Community concerning the powers of the Court of justice and the exercise of those powers shall apply to this Article and to Articles 40a and 40b.

Article 40a

1.   Member States which intend to establish enhanced cooperation between themselves under Article 40 shall address a request to the Commission, which may submit a proposal to the Council to that effect. In the event of the Commission not submitting a proposal, it shall inform the Member States concerned of the reasons for not doing so. Those Member States may then submit an initiative to the Council designed to obtain authorisation for the enhanced cooperation concerned.

2.   The authorisation referred to in paragraph 1 shall be granted, in compliance with Articles 43 to 45, by the Council, acting by a qualified majority, on a proposal from the Commission or on the initiative of at least eight Member States, and after consulting the European Parliament. The votes of the members of the Council shall be weighted in accordance with Article 205(2) of the Treaty establishing the European Community.

A member of the Council may request that the matter be referred to the European Council. After that matter has been raised before the European Council, the Council may act in accordance with the first subparagraph of this paragraph.

Article 40b

Any Member State which wishes to participate in enhanced cooperation established in accordance with Article 40a shall notify its intention to the Council and to the Commission, which shall give an opinion to the Council within three months of the date of receipt of that notification, possibly accompanied by a recommendation for such specific arrangements as it may deem necessary for that Member State to become a party to the cooperation in question. The Council shall take a decision on the request within four months of the date of receipt of that notification. The decision shall be deemed to be taken unless the Council, acting by a qualified majority within the same period, decides to hold it in abeyance; in that case, the Council shall state the reasons for its decision and set a deadline for re-examining it.

For the purposes of this Article, the Council shall act under the conditions set out in Article 44(1).'

C) General Provisions

10. The heading of Title VII shall be replaced by the following: 'Provisions on enhanced cooperation'.

11. Article 43 shall be replaced by the following:

'Article 43

Member States which intend to establish enhanced cooperation between themselves may make use of the institutions, procedures and mechanisms laid down by this Treaty and by the Treaty establishing the European Community provided that the proposed cooperation:

(a)   is aimed at furthering the objectives of the Union and of the Community, at protecting and serving their interests and at reinforcing their process of integration;

(b)   respects the said Treaties and the single institutional framework of the Union;

(c)   respects the *acquis communautaire* and the measures adopted under the other provisions of the said Treaties;

(d)   remains within the limits of the powers of the Union or of the Community and does not concern the areas which fall within the exclusive competence of the Community;

(e)   does not undermine the internal market as defined in Article 14(2) of the Treaty establishing the European Community, or the economic and social cohesion established in accordance with Title XVII of that Treaty;

(f)   does not constitute a barrier to or discrimination in trade between the Member States and does not distort competition between them;

(g)   involves a minimum of eight Member States;

(h)   respects the competences, rights and obligations of those Member States which do not participate therein;

(i)   does not affect the provisions of the Protocol integrating the Schengen *acquis* into the framework of the European Union;

(j)   is open to all the Member States, in accordance with Article 43b.'

12. The following Articles shall be inserted:

'Article 43a

Enhanced cooperation may be undertaken only as a last resort, when it has been established within the Council that the objectives of such cooperation cannot be attained within a reasonable period by applying the relevant provisions of the Treaties.

Article 43b

When enhanced cooperation is being established, it shall be open to all Member States. it shall also be open to them at any time, in accordance with Articles 27e and 40b of this Treaty and with Article lla of the Treaty establishing the European Community, subject to compliance with the basic decision and with the decisions taken within that framework. The Commission and the Member States participating in enhanced cooperation shall ensure that as many Member States as possible are encouraged to take part.'

Article 44 shall be replaced by the following Articles 44 and 44a:

'Article 44

1.   For the purposes of the adoption of the acts and decisions necessary for the implementation of enhanced cooperation referred to in Article 43, the relevant institutional provisions of this Treaty and of the Treaty establishing the European Community shall apply. However, while all members of the Council shall be able to take part in the deliberations, only those representing Member States participating in enhanced cooperation shall take part in the adoption of decisions. The qualified majority shall be defined as the same proportion of the weighted votes and the same proportion of the number of the Council members concerned as laid down in Article 205(2) of the Treaty establishing the European Community, and in the second and third subparagraphs of Article 23(2) of this Treaty as regards enhanced cooperation established on the basis of Article 27c. Unanimity shall be constituted by only those Council members concerned.

Such acts and decisions shall not form part of the Union *acquis*.

2.   Member States shall apply, as far as they are concerned, the acts and decisions adopted for the implementation of the enhanced cooperation in which they participate. Such acts and decisions shall be binding only on those Member States which participate in such cooperation and, as appropriate, shall be directly applicable only in those States. Member States which do not participate in such cooperation shall not impede the implementation thereof by the participating Member States.

Article 44a

Expenditure resulting from implementation of enhanced cooperation, other than administrative costs entailed for the institutions, shall be borne by the participating Member States, unless all members of the Council, acting unanimously after consulting the European Parliament, decide otherwise.'

14. Article 45 shall be replaced by the following:

'Article 45

The Council and the Commission shall ensure the consistency of activities undertaken on the basis of this Title and the consistency of such activities with the policies of the Union and the Community, and shall cooperate to that end.'

15. Article 46 shall be replaced by the following:

'Article 46

The provisions of the Treaty establishing the European Community, the Treaty establishing the European Coal and Steel Community and the Treaty establishing the European Atomic Energy Community concerning the powers of the Court of justice of the European Communities and the exercise of those powers shall apply only to the following provisions of this Treaty:

(a) provisions amending the Treaty establishing the European Economic Community with a view to establishing the European Community, the Treaty establishing the European Coal and Steel Community and the Treaty establishing the European Atomic Energy Community;

(b) provisions of Title VI, under the conditions provided for by Article 35;

(c) provisions of Title VII, under the conditions provided for by Articles 11 and 11a of the Treaty establishing the European Community and Article 40 of this Treaty;

(d) Article 6(2) with regard to action of the institutions, insofar as the Court has jurisdiction under the Treaties establishing the European Communities and under this Treaty;

(e) the purely procedural stipulations in Article 7, with the Court acting at the request of the Member State concerned within one month from the date of the determination by the Council provided for in that Article;

(f) Articles 46 to 53.'

Article 2

The Treaty establishing the European Community shall be amended in accordance with the provisions of this Article.

Article 11 shall be replaced by the following Articles 11 and 11a:

'Article 11

1. Member States which intend to establish enhanced cooperation between themselves in one of the areas referred to in this Treaty shall address a request to the Commission, which may submit a proposal to the Council to that effect. In the event of the Commission not submitting a proposal, it shall inform the Member States concerned of the reasons for not doing so.

2. Authorisation to establish enhanced cooperation as referred to in paragraph 1 shall be granted, in compliance with Articles 43 to 45 of the Treaty on European Union, by the Council, acting by a qualified majority on a proposal from the Commission and after consulting the European Parliament. When enhanced cooperation relates to an area covered by the procedure referred to in Article 251 of this Treaty, the assent of the European Parliament shall be required.

A member of the Council may request that the matter be referred to the European Council. After that matter has been raised before the European Council, the Council may act in accordance with the first subparagraph of this paragraph.

3.   The acts and decisions necessary for the implementation of enhanced cooperation activities shall be subject to all the relevant provisions of this Treaty, save as otherwise provided in this Article and in Articles 43 to 45 of the Treaty on European Union.

Article 11a

Any Member State which wishes to participate in enhanced cooperation established in accordance with Article 11 shall notify its intention to the Council and to the Commission, which shall give an opinion to the Council within three months of the date of receipt of that notification. Within four months of the date of receipt of that notification, the Commission shall take a decision on it, and on such specific arrangements as it may deem necessary.'

Bibliography

Andersen, S., and T. Burns
    1996   'The European Union and the Erosion of Parliamentary Democracy: A Study of Post-Parliamentary Governance', in S. Andersen and K. Eliassen (eds.), *The European Union: How Democratic Is It?* (London: Sage).

Armand, L., and M. Drancourt
    1970   *The European Challenge* (London: Weidenfeld and Nicholson).

Armstrong, K., and J. Shaw
    1998   'Integrating Law: An Introduction', *Journal of Common Market Studies* 36.2: 147-54.

Bailey, I.
    1999   'Flexibility, Harmonization and the Single Market in EU Environmental Policy: The Packaging Waste Directive', *Journal of Common Market Studies* 37.4: 549-71.

Bańkowski, Z., and A. Scott
    1998   'The European Union as an Essentially Contested Project', *European Law Journal* 4.4: 341-54.

Bellamy, R.
    2001   'The "Right to Have Rights": Citizenship Practice and the Political Constitution of the EU', in Bellamy and Warleigh (eds.) 2001: 41-70.

Bellamy, R., and D. Castiglione
    1997   'Building the Union: The Nature of Sovereignty in the Political Architecture of Europe', *Law and Philosophy* 16: 421-45.

Bellamy, R., and A. Warleigh
    1998   'From an Ethics of Integration to an Ethics of Participation: Citizenship and the Future of the European Union', *Millennium* 27.3: 447-70.

Bellamy, R., and A. Warleigh (eds.)
    2001   *Citizenship and Governance in the European Union* (London: Continuum).

Blondel, J., R. Sinnott and S. Svensson
    1998   *People and Parliament in the European Union: Participation, Democracy and Legitimacy* (Oxford: Clarendon Press).

Bulmer, S.
    1996   'The European Council and the Council of the European Union: Shapers of a European Confederation?', *Publius* 26.4: 17-42.

CEC (Commission of the European Communities)
    2001   *European Governance: A White Paper* (COM [2001] 428) (Brussels: European Commission).

Chaltiel, F.
  1998   'Le Traité d'Amsterdam et La Coopération Renforcée', *Revue du Marché Commun et de l'Union Européenne* 418: 289-93.
Chryssochoou, D.
  1994   'Democracy and Symbiosis in the European Union: Towards a Confederal Consociation?', *West European Politics* 17.4: 1-14.
  1997   'New Challenges to the Study of European Integration: Implications for Theory Building', *Journal of Common Market Studies* 35:4: 521-42.
  1998   *Democracy in the European Union* (London: IB Tauris).
  2000   'Meta-Theory and the Study of the European Union: Capturing the Normative Turn', *Journal of European Integration* 22.2: 123-44.
Chryssochoou, D., M. Tsinisizelis, S. Stavridis and K. Infantis
  1999   *Theory and Reform in the European Union* (Manchester: Manchester University Press).
Cini, M.
  2001   'The European Commission', in Warleigh (ed.) 2001: 41-60.
Closa, C.
  1998   'International Limits to National Claims in EU Constitutional Negotiations: The Spanish Government and the Asylum Right for EU Citizens', *International Negotiation* 3: 389-411.
Cram, L.
  1997   *Policy Making in the European Union: Conceptual Lenses and the Integration Process* (London: Routledge).
Cremona, M.
  2000   'Flexible Models: External Policy and the European Economic Constitution', in De Búrca and Scott (eds.) 2000: 59-94.
Curtin, D.
  1995   'The Shaping of a European Constitution and the 1996 IGC: 'Flexibility' as a Key Paradigm?', *Außenwirtschaft* 50: 237-52.
  1997   *Postnational Democracy: The European Union in Search of a Political Philosophy* (The Hague: Kluwer).
Dahrendorf, R.
  1979   'A Third Europe?', *3rd Jean Monnet Lecture,* European University Institute, Florence, 26 November 1979.
Dashwood, A.
  1996   *Reviewing Maastricht: Issues for the 1996 Intergovernmental Conference* (London: Sweet and Maxwell).
De Búrca, G.
  2000   'Differentiation Within the "Core"? The Case of the Internal Market', in De Búrca and Scott (eds.) 2000: 133-72.
De Búrca, G., and J. Scott (eds.)
  2000   *Constitutional Change in the EU: From Uniformity to Flexibility?* (Oxford: Hart).
De la Serre, F., and H. Wallace
  1997   'Flexibility and Enhanced Cooperation in the European Union', Paris: *Notre Europe* Research and Policy Papers No. 2/1997 – Revised Version.

De Witte, B.
    2000   ' "Old Flexibility": International Agreements Between Member States of the EU', in De Búrca and Scott (eds.) 2000: 31-58.

Devuyst, Y.
    1998   'Treaty Reform in the European Union: The Amsterdam Process', *Journal of European Public Policy* 5.4: 615-31.
    1999   'The Community-Method After Amsterdam', *Journal of Common Market Studies* 37.1: 109-20.

Dewatripont, M., F. Giavazzi, J. von Hagen, I. Harden, T. Persson, G. Roland *et al.*
    1995   *Flexible Integration: Towards a More Effective and Democratic Europe* (London: Centre for Economic Research).

Dooge, J., and P. Keatinge (eds.)
    2001   *What the Treaty of Nice Means* (Dublin: Institute of European Affairs).

Duff, A.
    1997a   *Reforming the European Union* (London: Sweet and Maxwell).
    1997b   *The Treaty of Amsterdam: Text and Commentary* (London: Federal Trust/ Sweet and Maxwell).

Edwards, G., and A. Pijpers (eds.)
    1997   *The Politics of European Treaty Reform* (London: Pinter).

Ehlermann, C.-D.
    1984   'How Flexible Is Community Law? An Unusual Approach to the Concept of "Two Speeds"', *Michigan Law Review* 83: 1274-93.
    1995   'Différenciation Accrue ou Uniformité Renforcée?', *Revue du Marché Commun* 3: 191-218.
    1998   'Differentiation, Flexibility, Closer Cooperation: The New Provisions of the Amsterdam Treaty', *European Law Journal* 4.3: 246-70.

Eriksen, E.O., and J.E. Fossum (eds.)
    2000   *Democracy in the European Union: Integration Through Deliberation?* (London: Routledge).

European Parliament
    2001   *Draft Treaty of Nice (Initial Analysis)* (Brussels: EP Directorate General for Committees and Delegations/Committee on Constitutional Affairs, PE 294.737).

Farrell, M., S. Fella and M. Newman (eds.)
    2002   *European Unity in Diversity: Challenges for the Twenty-First Century* (London: Sage).

FitzGerald, G., P. Gillespie and R. Fanning
    1996   'Britain: A Crisis of Identity', in P. Gillespie (ed.), *Britain's European Question: The Issues for Ireland* (Dublin: Institute of European Affairs).

Follesdal, A., and P. Koslowski (eds.)
    1998   *Democracy and the European Union* (Heidelberg: Spronger).

Forsyth, M.
    1981   *Unions of States: The Theory and Practice of Confederation* (Leicester: Leicester University Press).

Gaja, G.
    1998   'How Flexible Is Flexibility under the Amsterdam Treaty?', *Common Market Law Review* 35: 855-70.

George, S.
1994   *An Awkward Partner: Britain in the European Community* (Oxford: Oxford University Press, 2nd edn).
Gillespie, P.
1997   'The Promise and Practice of Flexibility', in Tonra (ed.) 1997: 49-64.
2001   'Enhanced Cooperation', in Dooge and Keatinge (eds.) 2001: 77-93.
Gowan, P., and P. Anderson (eds.)
1997   *The Question of Europe* (London: Verso).
Grant, C.
2000   'Where Might Enhanced Cooperation Be Used? The Case of Pillar II', Paper to Centre for European Reform/ESRC Seminar *The Governance of an Enlarged EU: What Scope Is there for Closer Cooperation?*, 29 June.
Groom, A.J.R., and P. Taylor (eds.)
1975   *Functionalism: Theory and Practice in International Integration* (London: University of London Press).
Haas, E.
1964   *Beyond the Nation State* (Stanford: Stanford University Press).
1968   *The Uniting of Europe* (Stanford: Stanford University Press).
1975   *The Obsolescence of Regional Integration Theory* (Berkeley: University of California Press.
Hall, P., and R. Taylor
1996   'Political Science and the Three New Institutionalisms', *Political Studies* 45: 936-57.
Hancock, J.R.
1941–44   *Plan for Action* (London: Whitcombe and Toombs Ltd).
Harrison, R.J.
1974   *Europe in Question* (London: Allen and Unwin).
1975   'Testing Functionalism', in Groom and Taylor (eds.) 1975: 112-38.
Hoffmann, S.
2000   'Towards a Common European Foreign and Security Policy?', *Journal of Common Market Studies* 38.2: 189-98.
Höreth, M.
1999   'No Way Out for the Beast? The Unsolved Legitimacy Problem of European Governance', *Journal of European Public Policy* 6.2: 249-68.
Hunt, J.
2001   'The European Court of Justice and the Court of First Instance', in Warleigh (ed.) 2001: 103-22.
Jachtenfuchs, M., T. Diez and S. Jung
1998   'Which Europe? Conflicting Models of Legitimate Political Order', *European Journal of International Relations* 4.4: 409-45.
Jeffery, C.
2000   'Sub-National Mobilization and European Integration: Does it Make any Difference?', *Journal of Common Market Studies* 38.1: 1-23.
Junge, K.
1999   *Flexibility, Enhanced Cooperation and the Treaty of Amsterdam* (London: Kogan Page).

Keating, M.
1999 'Assymetrical Government: Multinational States in an Integrating Europe', *Publius* 29.1: 71-86.
Kohler-Koch, B.
2000 'Framing: The Bottleneck of Constructing Legitimate Institutions', *Journal of European Public Policy* 7.4: 513-31.
Kohler-Koch, B., and R. Eising (eds.)
1999 *The Transformation of Governance in the European Union* (London: Routledge).
Kortenberg, H.
1998 'Closer Cooperation in the Treaty of Amsterdam', *Common Market Law Review* 35: 833-54.
Kuhn, T.
1970 *The Structure of Scientific Revolutions* (Chicago: University of Chicago Press, 2nd edn).
1977 *The Essential Tension: Selected Studies in Scientific Tradition and Change* (Chicago: University of Chicago Press).
Lamers, K.
1997 'Strengthening the Hard Core', in Gowan and Anderson (eds.) 1997: 104-16.
Laursen, F.
1997 'The Lessons of Maastricht', in Edwards and Pijpers 1997: 59-73.
Lord, C.
1998 *Democracy in the European Union* (Sheffield: Sheffield Academic Press).
Lyons, C.
2000 'Closer Cooperation and the Court of Justice', in De Búrca and Scott (eds.) 2000: 95-112.
MacCormick, N.
1993 'Beyond the Sovereign State', *Modern Law Review* 56.1: 1-18.
1999 *Questioning Sovereignty: Law, State and Nation in the European Commonwealth* (Oxford: Oxford University Press).
Maillet, P., and D. Vélo
1994 *L'Europe à Géométrie Variable: Transition vers l'Intégration* (Paris: L'Harmattan).
Marks, G., F. Scharpf, P. Schmitter and W. Streeck
1996 *Governance in the European Union* (London: Sage).
Miller, D.
1995 *On Nationality* (Oxford: Clarendon Press).
Milward, A.
1994 *The European Rescue of the Nation State* (London: Routledge).
Mitrany, D.
1933 *The Progress of International Government* (London: Allen and Unwin).
1944 A *Working Peace System* (London: Royal Institute of International Affairs, 2nd repr.).
1948 'The Functional Approach to World Organization', *International Affairs* 24.3: 350-63.

1965   'The Prospect of Integration: Federal or Functional?', *Journal of Common Market Studies* 4.2: 119-49.
1971   'The Functional Approach in Historical Perspective', *International Affairs* 47.3: 532-43.
1975   *The Functional Theory of Politics* (London: Martin Robertson).
Monnet, J.
1978   *Memoirs* (London: Collins).
Moravcsik, A.
1993   'Preferences and Power in the European Community: A Liberal Intergovernmentalist Approach', *Journal of Common Market Studies* 31.4: 473-524.
1999   *The Choice for Europe: Social Purpose and State Power from Messina to Maastricht* (London: UCL Press).
Moravcsik, A., and K. Nicolaidis
1999   'Explaining the Treaty of Amsterdam: Interests, Influence, Institutions', *Journal of Common Market Studies* 37.1: 59-85.
Neunreither, K.-H.
2000   'Political Representation in the European Union: A Common Whole, Various Wholes or Just a Hole?', in Neunreither and Wiener (eds.) 2000: 129-49.
Neunreither, K.-H., and A. Wiener (eds.)
2000   *European Integration after Amsterdam: Institutional Dynamics and Prospects for Democracy* (Oxford: Oxford University Press).
O'Neill, M.
1996   *The Politics of European Integration: A Reader* (London: Routledge).
Pedersen, T.
2000   'The EU after Amsterdam: Flexibility and Functionalism in Theoretical Perspective', *Current Politics and Economics of Europe* 9:2: 199-214.
Pentland, C.
1975   'Functionalism and Theories of International Political Integration', in Groom and Taylor (eds.) 1975: 9-24.
Peterson, J.
1994   'Subsidiarity: A Definition to Suit any Vision?', *Parliamentary Affairs* 47.1: 116-32.
1995   'Decision Making in the EU: Towards a Framework for Analysis', *Journal of European Public Policy* 2.1: 69-93.
Philippart, E.
2001   'The New Provisions on "Closer Cooperation": A Call for Prudent Politics', *European Community Studies Association Review* 14.2: 6-7.
Philippart, E., and G. Edwards
1999   'The Provisions on Closer Cooperation in the Treaty of Amsterdam: The Politics of Flexibility in the European Union', *Journal of Common Market Studies* 37.1: 87-108.
Philippart, E., and M. Sie Dian Ho
2000   'Flexibility and Models of Governance for the EU', in De Búrca and Scott (eds.) 2000: 299-330.
Rosamond, B.
2000a   *Theories of European Integration* (London: Macmillan).

2000b   'Theorising the European Union Past, Present and Future: On Knowl-
                edge, Discipline and "Thinking Thoroughly" about Integration Theory',
                Current Politics and Economics of Europe 9.2: 147-63.

Scharpf, F.
    1999   *Governing in Europe: Effective and Democratic?* (Oxford: Oxford Univ-
                ersity Press).

Schmitter, P.
    1996   'Imagining the Future of the Euro-Polity With the Help of New
                Concepts', in Marks *et al.* 1996: 121-50.

    2000   *How to Democratise the European Union... And Why Bother?* (Lanham,
                MD: Rowman and Littlefield).

Shackleton, M.
    2000   'The Politics of Codecision', *Journal of Common Market Studies* 38.2:
                325-42.

Shaw, J.
    1998   'The Treaty of Amsterdam: Challenges of Flexibility and Legitimacy',
                European Law Journal 4.1: 63-86.

    1999   'Postnational Constitutionalism in the European Union', *Journal of
                European Public Policy* 6.4: 579-97.

    2000   'Relating Constitutionalism and Flexibility in the European Union', in De
                Búrca and Scott (eds.) 2000: 331-58.

Sherrington, P.
    2000   *The Council of Ministers: Political Authority in the European Union*
                (London: Pinter).

Smith, M.
    2000   'Negotiating New Europes: The Roles of the European Union', *Journal of
                European Public Policy* 7.5: 806-22.

Stavridis, S., E. Mossialos, R. Morgan and H. Machin (eds.)
    1997   *New Challenges to the European Union: Policies and Policy Making*
                (Aldershot: Dartmouth).

Stubb, A.
    1996   'A Categorisation of Differentiated Integration', *Journal of Common
                Market Studies* 34.2: 283-95.

    1997   'The 1996 Intergovernmental Conference and the Management of
                Flexible Integration', *Journal of European Public Policy* 4.1: 37-55.

    2000   'Negotiating Flexible Integration in the Amsterdam Treaty', in
                Neunreither and Wiener (eds.) 2000: 153-74.

Taylor, P.
    1975   'Functionalism and Strategies for International Integration', in Groom
                and Taylor (eds.) 1975: 79-92.

    1978a   'A Conceptual Typology of International Organisation', in Taylor and
                Groom (eds.) 1978: 118-36.

    1978b   'Functionalism: The Theory of David Mitrany', in Taylor and Groom
                (eds.) 1978: 236-53.

    1983   *The Limits of European Integration* (Beckenham: Croon Helm).

    1993   *International Organisation in the Modern World* (London: Pinter).

    1996   *The European Union in the 1990s* (Oxford: Oxford University Press).

    1997   'Prospects for the European Union' in Stavridis *et al.* (eds) 1997: 13-42.

Taylor, P., and A.J.R. Groom (eds.)
1978   *International Organisation: A Conceptual Approach* (London: Pinter).
Therborn, G.
1997   'Europe in the Twenty-first Century', in Gowan and Anderson (eds.) 1997: 357-84.
Tindemans, L.
1976   'European Union: Report to the European Council', *Bulletin of the European Communities* Supplement 1/76, Luxembourg.
Tonra, B. (ed.)
1997   *Amsterdam: What the Treaty Means* (Dublin: Institute of European Affairs).
Tuytschaever, F.
1999   *Differentiation in European Union Law* (Oxford: Hart).
2000   'EMU and the Catch-22 of EU Constitution-Making', in De Búrca and Scott (eds.) 2000: 173-96.
Von Weizsäcker, R., J.-L. Dehaene and D. Simon
1999   'The Institutional Implications of Enlargement: Report to the European Commission', Brussels, 18 October.
Walker, N.
1998   'Sovereignty and Differentiated Integration in the European Union', *European Law Journal* 4.4: 355-88.
2000   'Flexibility within a Metaconstitutional Frame: Reflections on the Future of Legal Authority in Europe', in De Búrca and Scott (eds.) 2000: 9-30.
Wallace, H.
2000a   'Flexibility: A Tool of Integration or a Restraint on Disintegration?', in Neunreither and Wiener (eds.) 2000: 175-91.
2000b   'The Institutional Setting', in Wallace and Wallace (eds.) 2000: 3-38.
Wallace, H., and W. Wallace (eds.)
2000   *Policy-Making in the European Union* (Oxford: Oxford University Press, 4th edn).
Wallace, W.
1990   *The Transformation of Western Europe* (London: Pinter/Royal Institute of International Affairs).
Walzer, M.
1994   *Thick and Thin: Moral Argument at Home and Abroad* (London: University of Notre Dame Press).
Warleigh, A.
1998   'Better the Devil You Know? Synthetic and Confederal Understandings of European Unification', *West European Politics* 21.3: 1-18.
2000a   'History Repeating? Framework Theory and Europe's Multi-level Confederation', *Journal of European Integration* 22: 173-200.
2000b   'The Hustle: Citizenship Practice, NGOs and "Policy Coalitions" in the European Union: The Cases of Auto Oil, Drinking Water and Unit Pricing', *Journal of European Public Policy* 7.2: 229-43.
2001a   'Introduction: Institutions, Institutionalism and Decision Making in the European Union', in Warleigh 2001c: 3-21.
2001b   'Purposeful Opportunists? EU Institutions and the Struggle over European Citizenship', in Bellamy and Warleigh (eds.) 2001: 19-40.

2001c   *Understanding European Union Institutions* (London: Routledge).

2002   'Towards Network Democracy? The Potential of Flexible Integration', in
           Farrell *et al.* (eds.) 2002: 101-18.

Weale, A., and M. Nentwich (eds.)

1998   *Political Theory and the European Union* (London: Routledge).

Weiler, J.H.H.

1995   'Does Europe Need a Constitution? Demos, Telos and the German
           Maastricht Decision', *European Law Journal* 1.3: 219-58.

Wessels, W.

1998   'Flexibility, Differentiation and Closer Cooperation: The Amsterdam
           Provisions in the Light of the Tindemans Report', in Westlake (ed.) 1998:
           76-98.

Westlake, M. (ed.)

1998   *The European Union Beyond Amsterdam* (London: Routledge).

Wiener, A.

1998   *'European' Citizenship Practice: Building Institutions of a Non-State*
           (Oxford: Westview Press).

Wilson-Green, A.

1969   'Mitrany Re-read with the Help of Haas and Sewell', *Journal of Common
           Market Studies* 8.1: 50-69.

Wincott, D.

2001   'Looking Forward or Harking Back? The Commission and the Reform of
           Governance in the European Union', *Journal of Common Market Studies*
           39.5: 897-911.

Wind, M.

1998   'Flexible Integration: The European Union as a Polycentric Polity?',
           Paper to CORE Conference *Rethinking Constitutionalism in the EU,* 18–
           20 March.

Wistrich, E.

1991   *After 1992: The United States of Europe* (London: Routledge, rev. edn).

Young, H.

1998   *This Blessed Plot: Britain and Europe from Churchill to Blair* (London:
           Macmillan).

General Index

Index of Authors

UNIVERSITY ASSOCIATION FOR CONTEMPORARY EUROPEAN STUDIES
UACES Secretariat, King's College London, Strand, London WC2R 2LS, UK
Tel: +44 (0)20 7240 0206   Fax: +44 (0)20 7836 2350   Email: admin@uaces.org
www.uaces.org

UACES

University Association for Contemporary European Studies

The Association
- Brings together academics involved in researching Europe with representatives of government, industry and the media who are active in European affairs
- Primary organisation for British academics researching the European Union
- Over 600 individual and corporate members from Dept such as Politics, Law, Economics & European Studies, plus over 150 Graduate Students who join as Associate Members

Membership Benefits
- Individual Members eligible for special highly reduced fee for The Journal of Common Market Studies (JCMS)
- Regular Newsletter - events and developments of relevance to members
- Conferences - variety of themes, modestly priced, further reductions for members
- Publications, including the new series *Contemporary European Studies*, launched in 1998
- Research Network, and research conference
- Through the European Community Studies Association (ECSA), access to a larger world wide network
- Information Documentation & Resources eg: The Register of Courses in European Studies and the Register of Research into European Integration

Current Cost of Membership per annum
☛ Individual Members: £25.00   ☛ Associate (Student): £10.00   ☛ Corporate Members: £50.00

APPLICATION FOR MEMBERSHIP OF UACES
Please complete the appropriate details and return the entire form to the address above.

Last Name: _____   First Name: _____   Title (eg Mr): ___

Institution: _____

Faculty / Dept: _____

Institution Address: _____

_____

Work Tel No: _____   Work Fax No: _____

Home Tel No: _____   Home Fax No: _____

E-mail: _____

Address for correspondence if different: _____

_____

Where did you hear about UACES? _____

Signature and Date: _____

PTO TO COMPLETE PAYMENT DETAILS

UNIVERSITY ASSOCIATION FOR CONTEMPORARY EUROPEAN STUDIES
UACES Secretariat, King's College London, Strand, London WC2R 2LS, UK
Tel: +44 (0)20 7240 0206   Fax: +44 (0)20 7836 2350   Email: admin@uaces.org
www.uaces.org

PAYMENT DETAILS

☞ **TO PAY BY CHEQUE***

I wish to pay my membership subscription by cheque. Please make cheques payable to UACES, not King's College.

Please find enclosed a cheque (in pounds sterling) for:
❑ £25 (Individual)   ❑ £10 (Associate - Student)   ❑ £50 (Corporate)

* Please Note: we are no longer able to accept Eurocheques

☞ **TO PAY BY CREDIT/DEBIT CARD**

I wish to pay my membership subscription by (mark appropriate box):
❑ Visa   ❑ Mastercard   ❑ Eurocard   ❑ Switch   ❑ Solo

I authorise you to debit my Account with the amount of (mark appropriate box):
❑ £25 (Individual)   ❑ £10 (Associate - Student)   ❑ £50 (Corporate)

Signature of cardholder: _____   Date: _____

My Card Number is: ☐☐☐☐ ☐☐☐☐ ☐☐☐☐ ☐☐☐☐ ☐☐☐

Cardholder's Name and Initials*:_____ Cardholder's Title* (eg Mr): _____
*As shown on the card

Expiry Date: ☐☐☐   Start Date (if present*): ☐☐☐   Issue No. (if present*): ☐
*Usually for Switch and Solo cards

Cardholder's address and postcode (if different from overleaf):

_____

☞ **TO PAY BY STANDING ORDER* (UK Bank only)**
*This option not available for Corporate or Associate (Student) members

Please complete the details below and return to UACES. We will process the membership application and then forward this authority to your bank. This authority is not a Direct Debit authority (ie we cannot take money out of your bank account without your permission).

To (insert your Bank Name) _____ at (insert your bank address)

_____

_____ (insert Post Code) _____, UK.

Please pay to Lloyds Bank, Pall Mall Branch, 8-10 Waterloo Place, London SW1Y 4BE, UK, in favour of UACES, Account No. 3781242, Sort-Code 30-00-08, on the (insert date, eg 1st) _____ day of (insert month, eg June) _____ , the sum of £25 (TWENTY FIVE POUNDS) and the same sum on the same date each year until countermanded.

Signature: _____   Date: _____
Name: _____
Address: _____
Account No.: _____   Sort-code: _____

CES Ad1.doc